Self-Love for the Feminine Soul

Daily Affirmations, Guided Meditations, and Hypnosis for Healing Your Body and Mind

A 10 Week Program packed with activities to guide you to Self-Love

Written by: Elena Wright, Brandy Wells

Elena Wright © Copyright 2020 - All rights reserved.

The content contained within this book may not be reproduced, duplicated or transmitted without direct written permission from the author or the publisher.

Under no circumstances will any blame or legal responsibility be held against the publisher, or author, for any damages, reparation, or monetary loss due to the information contained within this book, either directly or indirectly.

Legal Notice:

This book is copyright protected. It is only for personal use. You cannot amend, distribute, sell, use, quote or paraphrase any part, or the content within this book, without the consent of the author or publisher.

Disclaimer Notice:

Please note the information contained within this document is for educational and entertainment purposes only. All effort has been executed to present accurate, up to date, reliable, complete information. No warranties of any kind are declared or implied. Readers acknowledge that the author is not engaging in the rendering of legal, financial, medical or professional advice. The content within this book has been derived from various sources. Please consult a licensed professional before attempting any techniques outlined in this book.

By reading this document, the reader agrees that under no circumstances is the author responsible for any losses, direct or indirect, that are incurred as a result of the use of information contained within this document, including, but not limited to, errors, omissions, or inaccuracies.

"And the world cannot be discovered by a journey of miles, no matter how long, but only by a spiritual journey, a journey of one inch, very arduous and humbling and joyful, by which we arrive at the ground at our own feet, and learn to be at home."

Wendell Berry (*The Unforeseen Wilderness*, 1971)[1]

Table of Contents

Note from the Authors 9

Introduction 15
    The Roots of Self-Love 17
    But Wait, What is Self-Love?................................18
    Let's Explore Femininity.......................................20
    Why Begin This Process?....................................22
    How to Use This Book 24
    A Guide to Self-Hypnosis 25
    Self-Love for the Feminine Soul: A Promise 27

Chapter 1 - Meet Yourself Where You Are, Right Now 29
    Exhale the Past 34
    Release the Future..35
    Accept the Present..36
    Week One Daily Affirmations 37
    Week One Healing Activities 38
    Week One Reflection 43

Chapter 2 - The First Steps Toward Self-Love 45
    Is This When We Start the Bubble Baths and Manicures?.........48
    From Punishment to Praise 50
    Take Care of Yourself 52
    Laugh a Little 52
    Week 2 Daily Affirmations 54
    Week 2 Healing Activities 55

Week 2 Reflection 59

Chapter 3 - Embrace the Vulnerability of Self-Care .. 61
Getting Comfortable with Vulnerability 63
The Vulnerability of Self-Care 66
Making Self-Care Tangible 69
Week 3 Daily Affirmations 71
Week 3 Healing Activities 72
Week 3 Reflection 76

Chapter 4 - Dive Deep to Learn Your Authentic Truth .. 77
Dig into Your Emotional Tendencies 79
Be Patient with Difficult Emotions 82
Honor Your Authentic Self 84
Week 4 Daily Affirmations 86
Week 4 Healing Activities 87
Week 4 Reflection 91

Chapter 5 - Cultivate Undeniable Self-Trust 93
Feel Confident in Belonging to Yourself 95
Acknowledge Your Strengths 100
Be Realistic and Follow Through 101
Week 5 Daily Affirmations 103
Week 5 Healing Activities 104
Week 5 Reflection 108

Chapter 6 - Protect Your Energy to Find Balance Between Rest and Activity 109
Self-Neglect in Action 111
Rest to Transform 115

Finding Ease in Your Activities 117
　　Week 6 Daily Affirmations 118
　　Week 6 Healing Activities 120
　　Week 6 Reflection 124

Chapter 7 - Create an Inner Voice of Kindness and Compassion 125
　　Make Peace With Your Inner Voice 128
　　Shifting Toward Compassion 130
　　Build a Flow of Kindness 133
　　Week 7 Daily Affirmations 134
　　Week 7 Healing Activities 135
　　Week 7 Reflection 139

Chapter 8 - Build a Self-Image of Strength and Resilience 141
　　What is Your Self-Image? 144
　　Restore Connections by Finding an Inner Friend 147
　　The Courage to Rewrite Your Self-Image 150
　　Week 8 Daily Affirmations 152
　　Week 8 Healing Activities 154
　　Week 8 Reflection 158

Chapter 9 - Celebrate Your Efforts and Bask in the Small Successes 159
　　True Self-Celebration 161
　　The Little Things Are the Big Things 164
　　Make it a Habit! 166
　　Small Steps, Big Impact 169
　　Week 9 Daily Affirmations..170

Week 9 Healing Activities 172
Week 9 Reflection 175

Chapter 10 - Breathe Self-Love into Your Routines Moving Forward 177
Explore Your Routines 179
Weave an Element of Self-Love 181
Acknowledge the Role of Society..186
Check in and Maintain Your Efforts 187
Week 10 Daily Affirmations 189
Week 10 Healing Activities 190
Week 10 Reflection 194

Conclusion: Tying it All Together..............................195
Revisiting Our Promises 197
Self-Love, Now 199
Let the Feminine Be 200
Where to Go From Here 201
Ending with a Promise 203

Resources 205

Note from the Authors

Self-love can be a difficult topic to get on board with. Believe me, I get that more than anyone. My journey with self-love began as an inner battle. I had been struggling with my mental health and confidence, and felt so much resistance toward myself. I was neglecting my inner self and forcing my outer self to behave in ways that didn't align with my true values. I was rejecting myself, judging myself harshly, and generally making life harder than it needed to be. Despite this extreme resistance, I knew something needed to change. I slowly started trying out different practices that settled my nervous system, brought me out of my head, and helped me find presence in my body. I started to see these practices as tools I could employ throughout the day to offer myself a bit of care, and begin to calm the inner critic.

The activities in this book are a mix of a few of the tools I've found most helpful in cultivating a consistent self-love practice. Affirmations, hypnosis, guided meditations, journal prompts, light physical activity, and clear visuals have all helped me find achievable ways to nurture myself, and work toward trusting myself again. Your toolbox will inevitably be unique to you, but I hope the provided activities will at least spark your curiosity, and encourage you to explore the possibilities for your own self-love practice.

I've chosen to incorporate this idea of the feminine soul because I've noticed some patterns between my own self-judgment and how society says we need to be as humans. Often, we are taught to reject certain sides of ourselves. Regardless of how we identify, we all possess some form of feminine energy, but something tells us we should hide these aspects of ourselves. Over time, I learned to be afraid of being vulnerable around friends. I started to hide my emotions and true feelings at work. I learned to use my generosity and nurturing qualities exclusively for pleasing others. I learned that only certain people are allowed to access femininity, and even then, it is only acceptable in certain situations.

I also noticed that the people in my life who come off as the most confident, brave, and joyful, are people who embrace their feminine energy. They express themselves freely, aren't afraid to discuss their true feelings, and don't let society dictate which parts of themselves they can reveal. They are the folks who embrace themselves fully in every setting, and never leave parts of themselves behind in order to fit in, please others, or edit themselves into a certain role. I feel that many of us keep certain aspects of ourselves hidden for fear of being perceived as weak, dramatic, emotional, or simply "too much." And frankly, I don't want to live like that anymore. I see embracing my feminine energy, and embracing my whole self, as an act of courage. I see it as a brave and necessary first step, a radical access point for building real self-love.

As you read the book, you'll see that I don't view self-love in quite the same way that it often gets portrayed. I don't believe we have to love ourselves before we can be loved by others. I know that self-love can be more challenging for some of us than others, because it was, and still often is, challenging for me. But that doesn't mean we have to wait until we get there in order to receive any love at all.

I think the whole point of self-love is learning that we are all deserving of love *now*. We can receive love in our lives, while also working toward loving ourselves better. It shouldn't have to be all or nothing. I also don't see self-love as this one-time, "achieve it, earn a trophy, and you are healed forever" thing. To me, self-love is a verb. An ongoing and necessary action, like exercising and nourishing our bodies, that we should practice every day of our lives.

My idea is, self-love comes in little gestures and steps that we carry out each day. We are all worthy of it now, and we can all achieve it if we just listen to our own needs.

If this is the first of our books you've read, please consider checking out *Hello, it's Confidence Calling* and *Modern Mindfulness*! *Hello, it's Confidence Calling* pairs well with this book, as many people exploring self-love also yearn for more confidence in their lives. Self-love starts as an internal shift, and cultivating more confidence is a way to bring the practice outward and into other areas of your life. Mindfulness is another excellent tool to employ in your self-love practice, as shifting your focus to the present helps remind you to be gentle with yourself in your thoughts and actions. We are continually creating new books to help our readers understand themselves better and cultivate an even better relationship with themselves.

Thank you for purchasing this book. Our readers are important to us, and we would love to hear from each of you. Please leave us a review to let us know what you think of our books, and share them with your friends!

Thank you for the support, and I sincerely hope you enjoy this exploration of self-love.

Disclaimer: Please note that the information provided in this book is for entertainment purposes only. The writings within this text are the opinions and advice of the authors, and we have made every effort to present accurate, reliable, and up to date information. No warranties of any kind are declared or implied. Readers acknowledge that the authors are not engaging in the rendering of legal, financial, medical, or professional advice. Please consult a licensed professional before attempting any techniques outlined in this book. Do not attempt any meditation or hypnosis exercises while driving or operating machinery. The advice provided in this book is not meant to precede or replace help from a medical or mental health professional.

Introduction

The concept of self-love has earned quite a bit of hype in recent years. Most of us are likely familiar with this idea that loving yourself should come first. It's that whole notion of putting on your own oxygen mask before assisting others. You have to love yourself before you can expect love in return, right?

Well, honestly, this common spin on self-love doesn't quite sit right with me.

For some of us, self-love doesn't come so easily.

Influencers and gurus spouting claims that self-love is the only ingredient missing from your life may bring up feelings of shame. If fear and shame control our thoughts on this topic, a lack of self-love may feel like yet another thing we are failing to achieve. And the notion that we are not loveable until we have learned to fully love ourselves is not only depressing, but harmfully inaccurate.

You deserve love and *are* loved, regardless of your current relationship with yourself. Even if you don't understand how to arrive at self-love, it is an important first step to acknowledge that you are already loveable, right now.

Yes, self-love is certainly a worthy goal, but my thought is that guilt-tripping ourselves may not be the best way to get there.

The Roots of Self-Love

Self-love is similar to happiness in some ways. They're both words we weigh down with endless expectations. They're also words we tend to place in the future.

"I will be happy when I earn X amount of money, when I pay off my debt, when I get my next big project done, or when I move into a new house."

"I will love myself when I get that promotion I have been waiting for, when my body looks how I want it to, when I find my dream partner, or when I kick the bad habit I've tried to beat forever."

Does any of this sound familiar?

Here's a bit of good news and bad news. Nothing outside of yourself is the ticket to achieving self-love. This means the roots of self-love are already inside of you, right now. This also means you can't expect changing your body, your job, your partner, or your address to automatically fill you with the love and happiness you seek.

But let's kick the guilt, shame, and fear to the curb before they have a chance to take over here. Self-love can be difficult. And it's especially difficult when society teaches us that our lives need to be perfect and also effortless. We need to be easygoing and down-to-earth, but also on top of every tiny detail of our lives. When these thoughts make up your mental dialogue, do you see how failure would be so much easier than success? Do you see how self-critique would be so much easier than self-love?

So let's adjust our expectations. Let's discover the roots of self-love inside of us, and rewrite a more realistic internal dialogue that helps them flourish and thrive.

But Wait, What *is* Self-Love?

If self-love isn't this impossible yet effortless thing we are all struggling to understand, how can we redefine it in a way that might provide relief rather than anxiety?

My definition is below; however, I encourage you to pause here and write out a definition of the kind of self-love you are striving for.

One of the most important things to realize is that this process will be different for everyone. You can take bits and pieces from this book and apply them to your experience, but ultimately, your experience is yours. Each piece, including your definition of self-love, should be crafted with language that resonates best for you.

My definition of self-love is nurturing and accepting yourself in the present moment, despite any urge to lean into shame, guilt, or fear. It is the act of continuing to stand up for yourself in this way over and over again, no matter how tempted you are to critique your own flaws. Self-love is not a state of eternal bliss that we arrive at one day. It is instead a repeated action. It is cultivating a toolbelt filled with steps you can take to accept your limitations, provide yourself space for expression and healing, and create more ease surrounding any difficulty you may be facing.

If you feel very far away from this definition, know that this is perfectly normal. So many of us struggle to love ourselves each day. This is because we have learned that paying more attention to our fears and flaws will keep us safe. Our fears tell us that we are lacking in some way, and every time we listen to that, we reinforce and strengthen this negative thought pattern.

Relax in your seat a bit. Fear doesn't get to take the driver's seat here. You've got the steering wheel. Turning inward, getting curious, and defining your own brand of self-love will help you build confidence and make the changes you've always wanted for yourself. Instead of seeing the process as slow and arduous, what if you tried to see it as luxurious and indulgent? Can you see the time spent as playful, fruitful, and inarguably necessary for your own healing? Bear with me.

Let's Explore Femininity

So we've begun to understand a bit more about self-love, but what about this concept of the feminine soul?

Self-love, and love in general, tend to be concepts we consider feminine in some way. I'd like to break up the notion that these ideas can only apply to a certain group of people. Every human, regardless of identity, exhibits some feminine qualities. By feminine qualities, I mean a call to creativity, expressing emotions, deeply connecting with the people you love, or tapping into your intuition. We all have feminine properties, and tapping into that wise, soft, and playful side of ourselves can be an extremely vulnerable endeavor.

Fear tells us we have to see everything as black or white. Anxiety encourages us to jump to the worst-case scenario. Shame tells us that our flaws make us unloveable. By tapping into the feminine elements of who we are, we can fight back against these urges to harden and put up walls. We can explore the idea that staying soft is an even more courageous approach to life's difficult moments. We can take a less harsh, less rushed approach to problem-solving and be a bit kinder to ourselves during the process. Embracing the gentle ease to be found in our feminine sides is a worthy path toward self-love.

Why Begin This Process?

Beginning the steps toward self-love may feel futile and pointless, and believe me, I get it. Whether you have already tried other programs or strategies with no luck, or you're just exploring this topic for the first time, let's take a look at some of the benefits that may encourage you to keep going.

Benefits of Cultivating Self-Love:

- Stop letting guilt and shame limit your ability to show up fully in your life
- Stop mistaking shyness and rigidity for your personality
- Stop letting the walls you've put up prevent you from expressing yourself creatively and freely
- Connect with others more authentically

- Stop letting self-doubt and self-sabotage prevent you from going after what you want
- Start living a life free from the physical and mental side effects of self-doubt and self-loathing
- Start exuding confidence, humor, and ease and allowing them to override fearful behaviors
- Rewrite your negative thoughts to stop feeling trapped inside your mind
- Develop a better relationship with your mind, learning to view thoughts objectively without becoming attached to them or controlled by them
- Accept and nurture yourself despite any mistakes or flaws
- Become more resilient when you do experience negativity or failure
- Learn to trust yourself and your intuition
- Develop routines that feel achievable and healthy

Does this sound like what you've been wanting? Know that this is all achievable. But also know that you are worthy of self-love now, even before you've begun.

You were born worthy of love.

And if any part of you is resisting that sentence, take note. Take it as a sign to dig deeper.

How to Use This Book

This book is designed as a ten-week program packed with affirmations, meditations, hypnosis, and many other activities to guide you toward a place of self-love. Each chapter expands upon a specific topic, and the accompanying activities allow you to put what you've learned into practice. Each day you can use a new affirmation as a focal point to return to if you get distracted by negative thoughts.

The idea is to go through this book one day at a time for the full ten weeks. Each day you can simply journal about or meditate on one of the affirmations, or try out one of the guided activities. Feel free to go at your own pace and craft an experience that feels healing for you. This is your experience, and it is important that you feel capable of guiding yourself in the way that works best for you. Make sure to answer the reflection questions before moving on to the next chapter, and continue like this throughout the book.

A Guide to Self-Hypnosis

This aspect of the book may be new to you, but that's okay. We've worked in consultation with a certified hypnotherapist to create easy self-hypnosis activities you can do at home. All you will need is a device for recording your voice, and a quiet, comfortable place to listen to your recording. You will record yourself saying the provided hypnosis script slowly and clearly. You are welcome to make adjustments to the script to include elements that are specific to your life. Then, you will get comfortable, close your eyes, and listen to the recording in a relaxed state.

We've chosen to incorporate hypnotherapy into this book because it helps spark quick and lasting change. This works because the relaxed state you enter allows hypnosis to move past the "thinking brain" that may be tempted to judge or resist the situation. Accessing the subconscious from a relaxed, nonjudgmental state helps the message sink in and leave a lasting impact. The scripts we've included use neuro-linguistic programming to create potent guided hypnosis exercises that help you cultivate a better relationship with yourself.

The act of listening to your own voice is an exercise in bringing the outer and inner versions of yourself together in harmony. Guiding yourself to a better mental state will build lasting self-trust and remind you that your inner self needs consistent attention and care.

Disclaimer: Do not attempt any of the self-hypnosis or meditation activities in this book while driving or operating machinery. Consult your health practitioner or mental health professional before attempting self-hypnosis. These activities are for self-discovery purposes, and not meant to substitute professional help from certified medical or mental health practitioners.

Self-Love for the Feminine Soul: A Promise

No matter how you have arrived on this page, I am glad you are here. You've taken a step toward cultivating self-love in the form of small daily actions. The activities in this book are designed to nudge your mind, body, and nervous system into a softer, more relaxed state. This gentle approach to nurturing and healing your mind and body will chip away at the walls you've built up, and help you discover the roots of self-love you've had inside you all along. This is not an external search, but rather, an uncovering of a truth that has always been.

I encourage you to pause again here and write down one promise to yourself related to your journey toward practicing self-love. This promise can be big or small. What is important is your intention to keep it. Making and keeping this first promise will start the process of building the self-trust needed to practice self-love.

My promise to you is that if you begin this journey from a place of curiosity, kindness, and openness, you will trigger the shift necessary to build a self-love practice.

Here are a few promises you may consider making to yourself now:

- I promise to complete this book within ten weeks.
- I promise to complete this book within one year.
- I promise to meditate on one self-love affirmation each day for one week.
- I promise to read chapter 1 now.
- I promise to adjust my self-love practice daily as it feels appropriate for my body and mind.
- I promise to be a little bit kinder to myself today.
- I promise to do one thing right now that is self-loving

Once you've decided on your promise, flip the page to get started!

Chapter 1

Meet Yourself Where You Are, Right Now

"Yesterday is gone. Tomorrow has not yet come. We have only today. Let us begin."
Mother Teresa (Goodreads, 2020)[2]

Imagine you have a big presentation coming up at work. You know you have the skills to nail it, but you've struggled with public speaking in the past. Those past scenarios keep playing out in your mind, and you begin to imagine yourself failing at this task as well. In this scenario, you are unknowingly allowing mistakes from the past and uncertainty in the future to impact your confidence, performance, and preparation in the present.

Do you notice that past scenarios shape the way you view yourself in the present?

Do you allow your mind to come up with negative stories about the future that consume your thoughts?

Do you use situations in the past or future to justify why you are not good enough?

Do you see how these thought patterns rob you of the ability to feel confident and fully accept yourself in the present?

It's safe to say the subconscious tendency for the mind to gravitate toward the past or the future is natural.

Whether you are frequently frustrated by this tendency, or you are just becoming aware of it, know that you are not alone. Our minds learn to focus on the stuff we choose to feed them. If we feed our minds stories of mistakes from the past or predictions of coming up short in the future, our minds will get really good at seeing these storylines in every scenario of our lives. This includes a self-love practice.

Before diving into the journey of cultivating self-love, it is important to develop some awareness surrounding your inner dialogue, and your willingness to accept yourself as you are, right now. It's time to retrain the brain to recognize these storylines of the past and future without becoming attached to them or mistaking them for the truth. As the past is behind you and the future is still uncertain, the only point of access to really accept yourself, get to know yourself, and learn to love yourself, is by embracing yourself in the present.

So how does this look in action? If your storyline is that you are dreadful at public speaking, start by noticing when this thought comes up, and how it makes you feel. Notice how long you dwell on the thought and how much power you give it. Maybe you even notice that your body tenses up, your palms get clammy, or your heart begins to race when thinking about a negative past experience. Practice disrupting this storyline with a kind thought, or reframing it in a way that moves from critical to accepting.

Here are some examples of how you can try reframing a self-critical thought regarding the past or future. The goal is to shift into a place of self-acceptance that allows you to release storylines and meet yourself in the present moment.

Self-Critical, Past/Future-Oriented Thought	Self-Accepting, Present-Oriented Thought
"I will fail at my public speaking assignment because I failed in the past."	"I have the tools I need to perform at my best and succeed at the tasks I am given."
"I won't amount to anything in the future because I never follow through with my goals."	"I am learning the skills to create goals that feel realistic and achievable for me. I trust myself to take one small step every day."
"I have experienced negative treatment in relationships in the past because I am unworthy of love and joy."	"I have been hurt in the past, and I allow myself to acknowledge and heal that pain. I am worthy of experiencing healthy, profound love and joy."
"I won't develop a lasting self-love practice because I can't envision a future where I feel good about myself."	"I have struggled with self-love in the past because of certain factors in my life that are not my fault. I can cultivate self-love that meets me where I am each day."

As this is chapter 1, we are naturally at the starting point of this self-love exploration, right? Actually, we cannot begin if our minds are stuck in the past, or we've mentally raced off into the future. This week is all about self-acceptance, so let's take a second to notice and accept the mental space we are in. Let's clear away any storylines that may be getting in the way of fully settling into the present moment, here together on this page.

Exhale the Past

Repetitive thoughts of the past can be quite tormenting if we let them dominate our minds. Not only are they limiting us, but they can also be a serious distraction from our daily tasks. Let's use the analogy of driving down the highway. The rearview mirror is there for a reason and can inform your decisions in the present. However, you would never put all of your focus on what is happening behind you. Doing so would jeopardize your driving performance and needlessly add risk to the situation. This is similar to what happens if we allow thoughts of the past to take over our minds and guide our behavior in the present. See the past as a tool, as useful information, and loosen your grip on any unproductive storylines that feel self-critical.

Exhaling the past means removing one barrier that is preventing you from accessing self-love in the present. This is a practice that takes time, and the activities throughout this book will help you get a little bit better at identifying this pattern each time it comes up. Soon, exhaling the past will become second-nature, and you will be able to identify and release negative past-oriented thoughts soon after they come up.

Release the Future

Releasing the future may be a bit trickier for some people. If you are frustrated with your current job, house, relationship status, financial situation, or relationship with yourself, it's difficult to understand how you can find self-love and acceptance in the present. You may be tempted to cling to the future in the hope that it will bring something better. However, by doing this, you are missing the opportunity to find even the smallest amount of joy, contentment, or connection in the present. You may be neglecting or abandoning your present self. If doing this becomes a habit, you won't know how to fully enjoy the things you wanted when they do eventually show up. Resisting uncomfortable present moments trains you to resist the present in general. This will leave you unable to accept and enjoy the good moments later on.

Releasing the future doesn't mean never making plans, being prepared, or working toward a better situation for yourself. It means releasing how much space the future occupies in your mind. The future is another barrier that prevents us from fully accessing self-love in the present. The promise that you will be worthy of self-love and acceptance "one day" robs you of the realization that you deserve both of these things right now.

Accept the Present

This week's activities will help you notice your thought patterns that remove you from the present and prevent you from accepting yourself as you are. When we settle the mind's tendency to steer away from the current reality, we can fully show up, right here and right now. We can begin to release distracting storylines. We can begin to uncover the ways that you can work toward self-love, no matter how far you are from "where you want to be."

This week's goal is to work toward accepting yourself, accepting your current situation, and accepting that even here, even now, you deserve to treat yourself well. With that notion in mind, let us begin.

Week 1 Daily Affirmations

As this is our first week, choose an affirmation and close your eyes. Ask yourself how you can incorporate this affirmation into your life today. You can use affirmations to help get your mind back on track if it gravitates toward negative thoughts. You can write the affirmation in a journal, write it on a piece of paper and stick it somewhere visible in your home or workspace, meditate on it, or use it in any other way you please.

"I release storylines of the past and future. I show up for myself in the present, over and over again."

"I exhale the past now. As I inhale, I feel profound love and acceptance for myself."

"I release my grip on the future. I am present."

"I am entering a state of unwavering self-acceptance."

"Each moment is a new opportunity to treat myself lovingly."

"I deserve to receive caring and nurturing treatment from myself."

"I am worthy of self-love, right here and now."

Week 1 Healing Activities

1. **Future Release Meditation:** Sit in a comfortable, upright position. Breathe deeply, in through your nose and out through your mouth. Imagine each of your worries about the future is a string attached to your chest. These strings

expand infinitely out in front of you, tugging on your chest and pulling you forward.

One by one, begin to snip each string with a pair of glowing, golden scissors. With each string you cut loose, you begin to feel lighter and more in control of your body. Stick with the visualization until you have cut away each worry and are free from the tugging of the strings. Notice how your body feels, newly released from the hold of the future.

2. **Action Step, Identify Your Storylines**: Find a journal or create a document you can use for writing prompts in this book. You may enjoy collecting other notes or discoveries you come across through this process.

At the top of the page, write one column labeled "past," and another labeled "future." In these columns, write down any negative, recurring thoughts you have about the past and the future.

Notice which thoughts come up first. Notice which list is longer. Make any notes about how you feel mentally and physically when these thoughts come up. Turn the page in your journal and write about how you plan to shift to the present when these thoughts come up.

3. **Acceptance Self-hypnosis:** Read this script before you begin, making any adjustments you'd like, to create a personal script for your recording. Once you've finished, record yourself saying the script slowly and clearly in an area with no background noise. Pause for at least ten seconds after each line of text, to give yourself time for visualization. Lie down in a comfortable position, relax your body, and replay the recording.

"Breathe in, and breathe out. Follow your breath as your stomach rises and falls.

Each time you breathe in, notice your eyelids getting heavier. Each time you breathe out, notice the muscles around your face relax more and more.

Complete five cycles of breath. On the fifth round, your eyes are closed and your body is deeply relaxed.

Notice the softness of your muscles now that they are relaxed. The relaxation continues to wash over you like a warm bath of water with each deep inhale and full exhale.

Allow yourself to float along in this warm bath. This warmth you feel is the present. In this bath you feel so profoundly safe and secure. You feel the current pull all thoughts of the past or future downstream and away from you. This state of being is so simple. Being present is so easy for you now.

As you sink deeper into relaxation, notice how easily you are accepting yourself and your current situation. Self-acceptance comes to you with ease, and you begin to extend acceptance to everything else in your world. You have found an ease in the present moment. You know you can tap into this feeling of self-acceptance at *any moment.*

Sinking even deeper into hypnosis, you let the warm water start to carry you now. You are so relaxed. You know you do not need to control the movement, or worry about where you are headed. You float along with ease like this, accepting your situation with the most confidence, and trusting your mind and body to provide you with everything you need in the present.

Offer yourself pure acceptance now. You are doing so well. This is a magnificent and powerful offering of self-love. You know that you can offer yourself this same acceptance and love at any time. You are starting to do this more already, just by being here now.

You come back to awareness now with ease. Start to come back to consciousness by wiggling your fingers and toes. Blink your eyes open and carry this acceptance and love with you as you continue your day."

Week 1 Reflection

1. Take some time to free-write your thoughts on how this week went. What did you enjoy? What was difficult? Which activities would you like to use again in the future?

2. Once you've reflected a bit about the week, come up with your own self-acceptance affirmation that sums up what you've learned. Try to pick a simple affirmation that can help you come back to the present whenever you get stuck on worries of the past or future.

Chapter 2

The First Steps Toward Self-Love

"Go back and take care of yourself. Your body needs you, your perceptions need you, your feelings need you. The wounded child in you needs you. Your suffering needs you to acknowledge it."

Thich Nhat Hanh

(*Reconciliation: Healing the Inner Child*, 2010)[3]

Take a second to think of a time when you've assumed the role of a caretaker. Maybe you have experience taking care of a child or training a puppy? If you were trying to explain a new rule, did the being in your care immediately behave without wiggling or protesting in some way? Chances are, the answer is no. Children love to test authority and choose their own way of doing things. Puppies may want to learn and gain your approval, but their little energetic bodies do not always cooperate. Both operate best when rewarded and praised for their progress. If you've had an experience like this, you know that while it may be frustrating, you are most successful in a caretaking role when you are patient, gentle, and kind. Do you think offering your mind this same care could be a useful approach?

Can you see how treating your mind like a child or small animal in your care may help you become more patient and kind with yourself?

If you consider yourself a good caretaker, are you treating yourself with the same nurturing approach

you offer others?

You know that neglect and harsh criticism don't help anyone progress, learn, and enjoy life. Can you see why these are not useful approaches to your relationship with yourself either?

Now that we've discussed the importance of returning to the present to develop self-love, you may be squirming in your seat a bit. This is normal. Over time, we've all developed one way or another to distract ourselves from thinking about things that cause us discomfort or pain. If your relationship with yourself is one of those uncomfortable things, you may be tempted to use one of your old strategies to flee. You may even be tempted to close this book altogether, but stick with me. This week we're going to ease into things and find a playful yet intentional approach to self-love.

Is This When We Start the Bubble Baths and Manicures?

This is the biggest stereotype about the topic of self-love, so it's worth dissecting a bit here. Self-love has become a cultural phenomenon, encouraging its practitioners to "treat themselves" to a face mask, massage, or luxurious soak in the tub. Yes, all of these things are great, but it's important that these efforts don't become yet another distraction or excuse for avoiding the difficult parts of life.

Cultivating fun self-love routines is worthwhile as long as they are backed up with awareness and intention, and are not simply a means of mental escape. Let's take a look at a few of the "cliché" self-love activities. The chart below demonstrates how the same activity can either be a distraction or a deliberate gesture of kindness, depending on the intention you put behind it.

"Cliché" Self-Love Activity	Distraction/ Self-Critical Mentality	Self-Loving Mentality
A Manicure	"I have been such a mess lately. Getting a manicure will at least give others the impression that I have it all together, and help me avoid my emails for a while."	"I have had a lot on my plate lately. I deserve to take a break to reflect, unwind, and engage in an activity that I know improves my mood."
A Bubble Bath	"I'm such a failure. I can't even take care of myself. At least a bubble bath will make it seem like I am treating myself well."	"I may have had a rough week, but I deserve to reward myself for the small wins I've had anyway."
Going to a Yoga Class	"I have been so lazy lately. The least I can do is make it to one yoga class. Plus, it will help me avoid the laundry piling up at home."	"I've felt off lately. Yoga helps me feel focused and calm, and I deserve to feel that way, no matter how productive I am."
Going on Vacation	My life is so overwhelming. I need to get away from my problems and toxic relationships for a while. Maybe I will never come back!"	"I know that I cannot run from my problems. Despite the inevitable chaos in life, I will allow myself to enjoy a bit of respite and return with a clear mind."

From Punishment to Praise

It can be quite shocking to realize that the same activity could either be self-loving or self-punishing, depending on the intention behind it. A yoga class can be a punishment if you are guilt-tripping yourself into it with thoughts of laziness or shame. It could also be a way of rewarding yourself for getting through a tough week, or an effort in shifting to a more loving inner dialogue. We'll discuss this inner voice more later on, but it's worth reflecting a bit now on the actions you take for yourself throughout the day. Are your actions, and the thoughts behind those actions, a form of punishment, or an act of praise and celebration? Do you go to the gym out of shame for your body, or to celebrate your strength and continue growing? Do you take a vacation to honor your own need for rest or adventure, or as a way to leave your problems behind temporarily?

You may already have a solid foundation for self-love routines in your life. This idea of intention can take them from activities rooted in negativity, insecurity, or fear, and shift them to deeply loving and nurturing habits. Checking in with your thoughts throughout the day can help remind you to steer back to self-love if you get distracted or enter a negative headspace. If you're unsure whether some activity in your life is an act of self-love, a distraction, or a form of self-punishment, ask yourself these questions to gain some clarity:

1. What is the intention behind this activity?
2. Am I operating out of love or fear?
3. After engaging in this activity, do I feel better or worse about myself?
4. Am I choosing to engage in the activity out of personal preference, or because I believe others want me to?
5. Does this activity feel like it is caring for and honoring my inner self, or causing more internal chaos?

Ask these questions, and come up with some of your own that you can use throughout the day. This can help you make sure that you are operating from a loving headspace. The act of checking in is very repetitive, but the more you develop this skill, the more natural it will begin to feel.

Take Care of Yourself

Going back to this idea that the "outer self" is the caretaker of the "inner self," we can dispel the idea that self-love has to be big gestures of treating ourselves. Instant gratification immediately feels great, but that feeling may be fleeting. Just like caring for a child, self-love isn't always giving gifts and treats. It can sometimes be more mundane, like organizing a shelf, getting your car washed, doing your taxes early, or washing your hair. The difference is, we may dread activities like these in the short term, but we know in the long-term, our future selves will be thankful, and we will begin to repair the relationship with ourselves. When we consistently take action to show up for ourselves, we begin to trust ourselves more. We learn that we can rely on ourselves for the daily care we need, so we begin to feel less mental chaos. Love and care begin to override fear and punishment. We slowly can begin to live better, more joyful lives.

Laugh a Little

Try not to take this process too seriously. A small dose

of humor goes a long way when it comes to developing a self-loving lifestyle. Learn to laugh at your self-punishing, fearful inner self. Coax that self into softening a bit. They have been cruel to you because they are hurting, but they want nothing more than some gentle love and care. Just like a child who is afraid of the monster under their bed, if they choose to laugh at their biggest fear, it begins to shrink and become more manageable.

Find the angle on self-love that feels right for you. This is the first step to finding routines and habits that you will stick with. Find ways of incorporating a playful, light-hearted mindset, so that the most vulnerable parts of yourself feel safe rather than frightened. These fun aspects of self-love are not the whole picture, but they are surely important and worthwhile. So, take that bubble bath, eat that slice of cake, paint your nails green, and laugh at your inner monster. Just remember to stay honest with yourself, keep checking in, and maintain an underlying intention of self-love.

Week 2 Daily Affirmations

As we take the first steps toward intentional self-love, remember to approach the process with a nurturing, caring mindset. Intention, care, celebration, and humor are all great ingredients to consider when forming self-love practices that work well for you. The affirmations for this week incorporate these elements to help you explore an intentional mindset and learn the way your inner self prefers to be treated.

Remember: Self-love is operating out of love, not fear. Self-love is celebration, not punishment or distraction. Self-love is strengthening your actions by putting a firm intention behind them. Self-love is learning to befriend your shadows and laugh when you stumble over them.

"I am my own best caretaker."

"I know, better than anyone, how I prefer to love and be loved."

"I am learning to befriend my inner self."

"The intention behind my self-loving actions is rooted in care and trust."

"I celebrate myself for who I am today."

"I can laugh when I stumble, and remain proud despite my imperfections."

"I am walking into a new chapter of life that is filled with self-love, joy, and confidence."

Week 2 Healing Activities

1. **Inner Love Meditation:** Find a comfortable position to sit with your eyes closed. Take a deep breath in, and exhale slowly and fully. Repeat this until your body feels fully relaxed. Now imagine yourself as a child, getting as specific as possible with the image, what you are wearing, where you are, and any other details that come up. Sit across from your inner child and hold their hands. Tell them you are here to care for them. Continue to sit with them for a few

minutes, coming back to the visual of your inner child sitting across from you each time your mind drifts away.

2. **Action Step**: Think of an activity you liked to do as a child. Maybe you loved playing outside, drawing, or playing a certain sport. Find time this week to incorporate a childhood hobby into your day. Let yourself find some joy in this activity no matter how foreign it feels to you now, simply honoring your inner child with a bit of play. Check in with your body during this activity, making sure to take care of it, note how it feels, and physically relax throughout the process.

3. **Self-Care Hypnosis:** Read this script before you begin, making any adjustments you'd like to create a personal script for your recording. Once you've finished, record yourself saying the script slowly and clearly in an area with no background noise. Pause for at least ten seconds after each

line of text to give yourself time for visualization. Lie down in a comfortable position, relax your body, and replay the recording.

"Breathe in, and breathe out. Allow your breath to be loud and full, making a sound like the waves of the ocean.

Just breathe in now, going to that relaxed place. Each time you breathe out, allow your shoulders to relax and lower a bit more.

Continue listening to your breath as if it were the waves of the ocean. Watch the tide roll in on the inhale, and out on the exhale. Each time the tide rolls in your feel yourself go deeper into a relaxed state.

Notice how effortlessly the tide rolls in and out. You smell the salt air and feel the wind rush along your skin. The sun warms you and you feel simply at peace.

You begin to walk along the shoreline, feeling the soft sand beneath your feet. Your body feels easy and gentle as you stroll along. As you continue to walk, you begin to see a figure in the distance. This figure looks familiar and innocent.

You continue walking toward the figure. With each step, you sink deeper into relaxation. The figure becomes more clear, and finally as you approach them, you realize this figure is you.

You are so relaxed, and you approach yourself with a gentle kindness. You embrace yourself and smile. You say to yourself, "You are doing so well. You are doing this exactly right." You continue walking now, side by side with yourself. You are so content as you just walk, listening to the ocean waves.

You are overcome with the belief that you are an innocent creature, worthy of care. You extend care and nurturing to the being walking next to you. You know that you can offer yourself this same care and love at any time. You are starting to do this more. Every time you hear this sound of the ocean breath, you will remember the innocent and worthy being that you are.

You come back to awareness now with ease. Start to come back to consciousness by wiggling your fingers and toes. Blink your eyes open slowly. Carry this feeling of nurturing self-care with you as you stand up and continue with your day."

Week 2 Reflection

1. Take some time to free-write your thoughts on how this week went. What did you enjoy? What was difficult? Which activities would you like to use again in the future?

2. Once you've reflected a bit about the week, come up with your own affirmation that sums up what you've learned about cultivating an intentional, nurturing self-love practice. Try to pick a simple affirmation that can help you find humor, celebration, and confidence in your daily life.

Chapter 3

Embrace the Vulnerability of Self-Care

"Vulnerability sounds like truth and feels like courage. Truth and courage aren't always comfortable, but they're never weakness."

Brene Brown (*Daring Greatly*, 2012)[4]

Have you ever been the odd one out in an argument? Imagine you are with a group of friends, and the group begins gossiping about a friend that isn't present. It makes you uncomfortable, but you feel self-conscious about speaking up. It's so much easier just to stay quiet, nod, and laugh along with your friends. In your head, you debate whether to stick up for your friend, voice your discomfort, and risk being shamed by the group. In this situation, being accepted socially comes at odds with acting in alignment with your values. This is a common dilemma in life, so use the example scenario as an opportunity to dig deeper.

Is the short-term gratification of social acceptance worth the long-term feeling of disappointment of not sticking up for yourself and your friend?

Do you see how taking risks to honor your values may be the more self-loving option in the long-run?

Do you think acting in alignment with your values, while vulnerable and sometimes scary, would lead

to more self-love in the long-run?

Choosing to stand up for our values will always be a vulnerable endeavor. Building a self-love practice is also a vulnerable endeavor. Both of these acts force us to forgo instant gratification and take a look at what feels true to us. We have to be okay with feeling soft, vulnerable, and open to the judgment of others. We have to be okay with going against the grain, slowing down, admitting we have reached our limits, or admitting we need help. The vulnerability of taking care of ourselves, or even admitting that we need care in the first place, may be why some avoid this topic. However, when we embrace self-care and vulnerability, they make our self-love practices so much richer.

Getting Comfortable with Vulnerability

Self-love is vulnerable because sometimes, the people around you don't actually *want* you to put yourself first. If you're used to prioritizing the desires of others before your own, choosing to honor yourself might disrupt old relationship dynamics. At this stage, you need to be ready for two things to happen:

1. **You need to be ready to be challenged for your decision to choose yourself.**
2. **You need to be ready to stick with the decision, even if it causes a disruption or conflict.**

Though sometimes this can cause disruption, usually, we magnify the impact in our minds. No, choosing yourself doesn't mean deliberately hurting the people around you. It means having the courage to think about what you want, and honor yourself by making the desire known. This can play out in even the simplest of scenarios. Imagine you are making dinner plans with a group of coworkers. The group is trying to decide between burgers, tacos, or sushi. You've been wanting to try the sushi place for months, and don't care for the other two options. It would be so simple to voice this, but you don't want to sway the group, and you know you can find something on any menu. We tend to think people prefer friends that are easygoing, but in this case, most people would actually prefer to know your preference.

This example may seem silly, but even the small decisions in our lives add up. Each time you take the risk of voicing your preference, no matter how simple, you get to know yourself a bit better. You tell yourself that your preferences matter. You take a bit of power back in your life, and your inner self feels the love in these gestures. Here are a few more examples of small gestures that can actually help you practice being vulnerable and voicing your truth:

- Telling your partner you'd like to go on a date this week
- Asking to take a short break to drink some water during a meeting
- Telling your family you need half an hour of alone time in the evenings
- Leaving a party when you are ready to go, even if you're the first one to leave
- Telling your friends that you would prefer not to participate in gossip

- Asking for help with a household chore
- Asking a friend for advice
- Asking to sit outside if the noise in the restaurant is bothering you

As you can see, there are actually quite a few opportunities throughout the day for you to stick up for yourself. Sometimes the small desires we have can feel so meaningless that we don't even give them a second thought. If you feel like you don't even know your own preferences sometimes, tuning into these small moments can help you strengthen that inner knowledge. Getting comfortable with vulnerability will help you get to know and learn to trust yourself. Each time you honor your preferences, you strengthen the message of self-love that you are sending to your inner self.

The Vulnerability of Self-Care

Strengthening your ability to be vulnerable is a key ingredient for consistent self-care. Self-care is taking deliberate action to nurture your inner self. If you have been hard on yourself in the past, it can also be vulnerable for your inner self to acknowledge and accept new gestures of self-love. Just like a child, your inner self may be skeptical of something they haven't yet learned to trust. If you feel resistance to developing a self-love practice, this could be why. You may find that you are afraid to trust yourself. Maybe trying something new led you to criticize yourself harshly in the past. It takes time, patience, and consistency to repair this relationship with yourself, but I think if you've read this far, you know this endeavor is worthwhile.

In order to be vulnerable, we need to feel safe to be our authentic selves. On the path to self-love, this means learning to feel at home in our own skin. Maybe your body and mind have not felt like the safest places to be in the past. Maybe you are hard on yourself. Maybe you endure mental or physical stress to punish yourself for not being good enough. Maybe you suppress certain emotions or try to numb any pain you feel. These are all ways we can teach ourselves that our bodies and minds are not safe places. Once we learn this, we accept it as a fact. It becomes subconscious, and we don't give it much thought. It takes some undoing and relearning to get to a place where we feel safe in our bodies and minds again. Here are a few examples of ways you can begin to feel more comfortable and safe within your body and mind:

Action:	The message that sends to your inner self:
Do some stretches before bed.	I love my body and believe that it deserves to feel relaxed and clam.
Journal some positive thoughts about yourself.	I may not be perfect, but I love myself anyway. I deserve a mind that loves me rather than punishes me.
Take some time to enjoy a nice drink with no screens or distractions.	I deserve to create a calming, restorative space to relax my body and mind.
Plan a morning routine that you are excited to wake up for.	My needs are unique to me. They are worth learning and honoring. I am willing to do what it takes to trust myself again.

For some people, it can be challenging to see the point in forming new habits, putting in a bit of extra effort, and sticking with something you may feel you don't have time for. Trust me, I get it. But these tiny actions are where big change can happen. Learn to see your body and mind as your home. Build the home up with kind thoughts, loving care, and calming routines. Put your preferences at the forefront, and show yourself that this is the new way the house is run. Slowly, you'll begin to feel safe opening up and living fully within your own space.

Making Self-Care Tangible

You may not always relate to the examples I give when discussing vulnerability and self-care, and that's okay. With any program like this, it is important for you to take what feels right, leave what doesn't, and begin learning the skills to map out your own self-love practice. I want you to be able to walk away with your own ideas about what feels right for your body, mind, and inner self. Take the lessons you find here and get as specific as you can with your own relationship with yourself. At the end of the day, it is you who has to live in the home you create in your body and mind. You need to build it to meet your needs and your needs alone. Here are a few ideas for getting specific with your self-care. Take these ideas and morph them into your own personal mind-map for how to add a bit of self-care into your day.

- I will wake up at 7:00 am and drink a glass of water while I meditate.
- I will take five minutes each evening at 9:00 pm to breathe and drink some tea.
- I will take five minutes during my lunch break to stretch my muscles before going back to work.
- I will swap scrolling through social media with ten minutes of reading before bed.
- I will journal each evening to practice creating a positive mental space.
- I will practice listening to my gut reaction instead of dismissing it when asked to make decisions in a group setting.
- I will listen to my nervous system when I become anxious in social settings, and learn to make adjustments to promote physical and mental calm.

These suggestions are just to give you an idea of how you can create tangible self-care habits in your daily life. It is important to go from the idea of loving yourself to taking regular self-loving actions that feel good to you. Feel free to jot some of your ideas down in your journal before moving forward with this week's activities.

Week 3 Daily Affirmations

This week's affirmations are all about the importance of leaning into vulnerability to create a consistent self-love practice. Allow these affirmations to help you as you begin building a nurturing home within your own mind and body.

"In vulnerable moments, I know that I have my own back."

"I take daily steps to show myself the care and love that I deserve."

"I honor my values in each moment of my life."

"I always choose the option that honors my present self and nurtures my future self."

"I am creating a home within my body and mind that feels safe and loving."

"I live a life abundant in caring, nurturing activities."

"My thoughts are becoming more naturally caring and self-loving each day."

Week 3 Healing Activities

1. **Inner Home Meditation:** Find a comfortable position to sit with your eyes closed. Take a deep breath in, and exhale slowly and fully. Repeat this until your body feels fully relaxed. Now imagine you are sitting in a cozy room, the details of the room do not matter, but you feel safe, relaxed, and fully open. Allow yourself to create a home that feels exactly like you want it to. Once you have relaxed into your home,

repeat the phrase in your head: I am safe here. I am safe here. I am safe here. Continue to repeat the phrase and breathe for a few minutes, acknowledging that your body and mind are a loving and nurturing space for you to dwell.

2. **Self-Care Action Step**: Remember that list of specific self-care steps we created at the end of the chapter? If you didn't create one, take time to jot down a few very specific ideas for self-care. This week, try to incorporate just one of these steps into your daily routine. Maybe you stretch for five minutes in the morning, or go on a short walk during your lunch break, or read for ten minutes in the evening. Try to stick with it, taking it just one day at a time. Notice how you feel after a week of this new habit.

3. **Self-hypnosis:** Read this script before you begin, making any adjustments you'd like to create a personal script for your recording. Once you've finished, record yourself saying the script slowly and clearly in an area with no background

noise. Pause for at least ten seconds after each line of text to give yourself time for visualization. Lie down in a comfortable position, relax your body, and replay the recording.

"Begin to breathe in, slowly observing as your lungs fill with fresh air. Breathe out and release any muscle tension you notice in your body.

Place your hands on your belly in a way that feels natural. They create a space where your belly can rise and fall with ease. This comforting gesture helps you sink even deeper into relaxation.

Just enter that inner space now, going to that inner home that opens up with such ease. You feel as safe and secure as your stomach does, rising and falling beneath your hands.

Each time you breathe in, you notice your inner world expanding. Each time you exhale, you relax even deeper, surrendering to the safety you feel in your own beautiful space.

A flickering flame appears in front of you. It dances as you breathe, and warms you from within. You are overcome with the knowledge that no matter how deeply you breathe, no matter how uncertain you feel, this flame will not be extinguished.

You feel this flame warming your belly, kept safe by your protective hands. You are so relaxed by this safety and warmth. You are beginning to trust this space more and more.

You realize that the safety you feel here, the warmth, and the beautiful light, are growing stronger the longer you dwell in this space. The more time you spend in this loving home, the more you accept it and allow it to protect you.

You know now that honoring your values and staying true to yourself are all about this sense of home. You know this space is always here for you. You know it will protect you, so there is no need to feel unsure. You accept this space and trust it completely now.

Carry the warmth you feel all the way back to a sense of awareness. Start to come back to consciousness by wiggling your fingers and toes. Open your eyes, and carry on with your day, knowing you carry home with you wherever you go."

Week 3 Reflection

1. Take some time to free-write your thoughts on how this week went. What did you enjoy? What was difficult? Which activities would you like to use again in the future?

2. Once you've reflected a bit about the week, come up with your own self-care affirmation that sums up what you've learned about the value of being vulnerable. Try to pick a simple affirmation that can remind you of the importance of staying true to your values.

Chapter 4

Dive Deep to Learn Your Authentic Truth

"Only the truth of who you are, if realized, will set you free."

Eckhart Tolle (*A New Earth*, 2005)[5]

Think back to a time when anger or sadness overcame you. Maybe you find that these emotions frequently overwhelm you and cause you pain. Perhaps one time you got so angry that you shouted at someone you loved, slammed a door, stormed out, or made another rash decision that you regretted later. We often allow the pain of emotions like anger and sadness to make our decisions for us. We become so uncomfortable that we lash out, run away, or become paralyzed and unable to address the problem. This happens to all of us at some point, but usually, the aftermath leaves us feeling regretful. Maybe we hurt a loved one, or maybe we even hurt ourselves. Avoiding pain only causes us more pain, so what if we could train ourselves to approach these situations differently?

Do you notice any tendencies in yourself when dealing with emotions like anger and sadness?

Diving into these tendencies may be scary, but do you think it would be worth it if it meant you could stop repeating them?

Is the discomfort of sitting with yourself during stressful situations or overwhelming emotions worth enduring for the sake of self-love?

This topic may lead to more resistance than you have felt in previous chapters, and that's okay. Just remember that developing negative tendencies is normal. We do this to minimize the pain we feel in certain situations. It is just a side-effect of being human. However, sometimes we need to check-in with our tendencies to see whether they are helping us or hurting us. We may have outgrown behaviors that were once helpful for us somehow. Be patient with yourself this week; it has the potential to provide a bit of relief and deepen your self-love practice profoundly.

Dig into Your Emotional Tendencies

A big part of self-love is rediscovering the positive aspects of yourself that you may have stopped seeing. However, once you develop a less critical, more curious and loving relationship with yourself, it is important not to bypass the elements that may be holding you back. If we gravitate toward the positive and overlook the negative completely, we miss out on significant and crucial opportunities for growth. We also deny ourselves the opportunity to accept ourselves fully. It's time to trust yourself to examine negative tendencies without judgment. This, in itself, is an act of self-love.

Let's explore some examples of negative tendencies to help you pinpoint what yours may be:

"Negative" Emotion	Behavior in Response to the Emotion
Anger	Anger Lashing out, shouting at people, running away from the situation, saying things you don't mean, throwing things or slamming doors, becoming unable to see a middle ground
Sadness	Numbing the emotion with unhealthy eating or drinking habits, suppressing the feeling, acting out angry behaviors instead of addressing sadness, putting up walls, surrounding yourself with people or activities to distract you from feeling sad
Guilt	Harshly critiquing yourself, shaming yourself relentlessly, replaying scenarios in your head, hiding from certain people or situations
Jealously	Comparing yourself to others, thinking negative thoughts about yourself, withdrawing socially, putting down other people, engaging in gossip
Self-doubt	Putting yourself down, critiquing yourself mentally and physically, isolating yourself, judging or putting down other people, withdrawing socially, pretending to be someone you are not, acting out of alignment with your values

I've put the word "negative" in quotations intentionally here. Sure, some emotions are more painful than others, but all emotions are important, and we don't get out of experiencing any of them. The way we behave when we feel certain emotions provides us with useful information if we allow ourselves to see it. If you can be patient and view how you respond to certain emotions, you can learn key information for moving forward and taking better care of yourself.

Be Patient with Difficult Emotions

The fun and easy sides of self-love are understandably more pleasant to engage with. However, sifting through the more difficult feelings and emotions is just as, if not more important. If you've made it this far, you have shown yourself that self-love is a worthy endeavor. Don't stop now. The more unpleasant emotions may feel good to avoid in the short-term, but addressing the way we process them can help us get to a much healthier, happier, and more self-loving place.

The key ingredient for working through this phase of the process is patience. If you can be patient with yourself, the abilities to change and grow a solid self-love practice are well within reach. Take some time to write out some of your tendencies and how you want to work on changing them. If you are satisfied with the way you respond to a certain emotion, write out why. Here are some examples of how this may look:

- **When I am angry**, I often shout at my partner and say hurtful things I regret later. **I want to work toward responding to anger by** taking a break to leave, breathe, and come back to address the problem with a clearer mind and calmer body.
- **When I am sad**, I often try to drown out the emotion by burying myself in work and socializing. **I want to work toward responding to sadness by** giving myself time and space to slow down, cry if I need to, and fully process the emotion before diving back into work.
- **When I feel self-doubt**, I often withdraw from social settings and isolate myself. **I want to**

work toward responding to self-doubt by taking a break to gather my thoughts, remind myself that I am worthy and loved, and spend time with people who help me feel seen and heard.

No matter what your tendencies are, do not shame yourself or get frustrated. You are the way you are for a reason, and now you can take back some control and steer yourself toward behaviors that you would prefer to have. A bit of patience and effort will go a long way, and you will eventually be glad you took the time to sit with your difficult emotions and tendencies.

Honor Your Authentic Self

Honoring your authentic self is more than just examining difficult emotions. Your responses to positive emotions are worth exploring, as well. Do you allow yourself to feel happiness completely? Do you cover up feelings of excitement or love because you don't want to appear silly or weak? Showing up as your true self when feeling positive emotions can feel vulnerable as well. Maybe we don't want to show people the things that make us happy, because we are afraid they will get taken away. Maybe we don't want to express love, because we are afraid we will be rejected. Take some time to explore your positive emotions in your journal as well. Here are some examples of how this may look:

- **When I am happy**, I often minimize my own joy by focusing on my shortcomings. **I want to work toward responding to happiness by** allowing myself to feel happy, and tell others that I am happy without judging myself.
- **When I feel love**, I often suppress the feeling or change the subject altogether. **I want to work toward responding to feelings of love by** expressing it outwardly through loving words and actions.
- **When I feel hope**, I often talk myself out of it by thinking negative thoughts. **I want to work toward responding to hope by** writing down the thought that made me feel hopeful and putting energy toward thinking similar positive

thoughts.

No matter how uncomfortable you feel exploring the behaviors you want to change, I hope you realize that the discomfort is not permanent. Diving deep, sitting with the discomfort, and being patient with yourself will lead toward meaningful change in time. When you take this time to get to know yourself better and guide yourself toward healthier behaviors, you show yourself the self-love you have been longing for.

Week 4 Daily Affirmations

The affirmations for this week encourage you to be patient, focus on self-discovery, and know that you can release negative behaviors. Even if you have always thought your personality was fixed, you can always change, and self-love will help you get there. Be gentle with yourself, allow it to take the necessary amount of time, and open up to your authentic self.

"I am patient with myself through difficult emotions."

"I honor my truth in all areas of life."

"My path to self-discovery is fruitful, joyful, and never-ending."

"My authenticity shines because I love myself well."

"I learn from my negative behaviors and release them readily."

"I know myself intimately and love myself fully."

"I release anything I have been carrying that is not in alignment with my truth."

Week 4 Healing Activities

1. **Authentic Self Meditation:** Find a comfortable position to sit with your eyes closed. Take a deep breath in, and exhale slowly and fully. Repeat this until your body feels fully relaxed. Imagine you are sitting beneath many colorful layers of

fabric. These fabrics feel heavy and weigh you down. One by one, a force begins pulling the fabrics away. With each fabric removed, you feel lighter, you can breathe more fully, and your inner light can shine brighter. Continue the meditation until the last fabric is pulled away, revealing your inner light and allowing you to feel so light that you begin floating. Your authentic self is present, as it always was, and is now free to shine its brightest.

2. **Emotions journaling action step**: Pick one difficult emotion (e.g., sadness, anger, jealousy) and one emotion you enjoy (e.g., happiness, love, gratitude). Each day, keep a list of times these emotions came up, and how you responded to them. At the end of the week, see if any patterns emerge regarding your behaviors. Does observing these behaviors help you feel like you could change them? Did noticing any joyful moments allow you to enjoy them more fully?

3. **Authenticity Self-hypnosis:** Read this script before you begin, making any adjustments you'd like, to create a personal script for your recording. Once you've finished, record yourself saying the script slowly and clearly in an area with no background noise. Pause for at least ten seconds after each line of text to give yourself time for visualization. Lie down in a comfortable position, relax your body, and replay the recording.

"Close your eyes and breathe easily, in through your nose and out through your mouth.

Place your hands on your heart, feeling the warmth and allowing it to radiate through your chest.

The warmth in your chest is starting to become bright and vibrant. Your chest is glowing bright green, like a beautiful, lush forest. You feel your chest rise and fall as you sink deeper into relaxation.

Each time you breathe in, you notice the light in your chest growing brighter. Each time you exhale, you relax even deeper, and watch as the light catches difficult emotions, allowing them to glow bright too.

This bright green light is transmuting everything into a warm and glowing positive force within you. You know you are so much more than your behaviors. You know this glowing light is uncovering your authentic truth.

The light is melting away all the walls and masks you've held up for so long. You are so relaxed by the knowledge that you are free from these things. You are allowing your authentic truth to show itself. This is an effortless, joyful, vibrant feeling.

You can see that this light, your authenticity, has the power to heal your body and mind. As you let this light completely relax your body, you notice it also smoothing out and relaxing your mind.

You see that there was never anything between you and your authentic self. You easily see your authentic truth. You know you can operate as this most authentic, confident, and truly happy version of yourself at all times.

Allow this beautiful green light to linger as you tap back into awareness. Start to come back to consciousness by wiggling your fingers and toes. Open your eyes and take a deep breath, knowing the most authentic version of you is still here with you now."

Week 4 Reflection

1. Take some time to free-write your thoughts on how this week went. What did you enjoy? What was difficult? Which activities would you like to use again in the future?

2. Once you've reflected a bit about the week, come up with your own self-discovery affirmation that sums up what you've learned about digging deep and uncovering the truth within yourself. Try to pick a simple affirmation that can help you stay patient when dealing with difficult emotions.

Chapter 5

Cultivate Undeniable Self-Trust

*"You do not have to be good.
You do not have to walk on your knees
for a hundred miles through the
desert, repenting. You only have to let the
soft animal of your body love what it loves."*

Mary Oliver (*Wild Geese*, 2004)[6]

Imagine it is the start of a new year, and it's time to pick a New Year's resolution. Maybe you try to start a new habit of working out twice a week. You start out strong, going twice a week for a few weeks in January. However, by the time February rolls around, you have to go to the mechanic, or come down with a cold, so you miss a week. After missing that week, you start letting smaller things be excuse enough to miss your workouts. It's too cold outside, or you're tired, or you have too many other chores to tackle. While it's healthy not to be too harsh on yourself about falling short here and there, what do you think this habit is doing for your relationship with yourself?

When you set goals that are unrealistic or unaligned with your values, do you trust yourself to follow through?

When you don't follow through with a goal you've made for yourself, do you think this impacts how much you trust yourself in other areas of life?

Instead of creating big, unsustainable goals, do you

think one small, consistent goal could be enough to help you build trust in yourself again?

This week is all about trusting yourself, why it's challenging, and how to build self-trust in small, loving, and intentional ways. If you are unsure about your level of self-trust, know this. You have made it to chapter 5 of this book. No matter how long it took you to get here, you trusted yourself to work through each chapter in order to build self-love, and now here you are. Allow this to be a moment of celebration, a moment to acknowledge that you must already possess some level of self-trust. Now let's dig in to discover more, and see how we can build upon this feeling.

Feel Confident in Belonging to Yourself

You could say self-trust is the act of belonging to yourself. When we are children, we may feel as though we belong to our parents. We consult them when we have problems, they help us with homework, and they plan out daily schedules for us. So in adulthood, it's important to learn to offer yourself the same support.

You may use the parent-child example as a guideline, or you may be starting from scratch. Either way, learning to belong to yourself is a shift out of self-doubt, and into self-trust. Let's take a look at a few examples of a self-doubting mindset, and how it compares to a more self-trusting approach.

Self-Doubting Mindset	Self-Trusting Mindset
I have a big decision to make, and I am unsure what to do. I will ask everyone I know what they think and make my decision based on their feedback.	I may consult a few important people in my life when making a big decision. However, I know how to reflect internally, listen to my preferences, and trust that I know what is best for myself.
When someone makes a comment that doesn't sit right with me, I keep quiet, knowing I am probably the only one that feels that way.	When something doesn't sit right with me, I stand up for myself, feeling confident that I made the right choice and honored my values well.
I set goals that I have seen other people set. If they can keep them, why shouldn't I be able to?	I check-in with my preferences, needs, and abilities, and set goals that I see as achievable for me personally.
I use excuses to justify falling short in life, but secretly I shame myself for not being good enough.	I know sometimes I will fall short because I am human. I do not shame myself for this, but instead, use it as an opportunity to check-in and reassess my expectations.
My thoughts about myself are usually negative and critical.	My thoughts about myself may be critical at times, but I know how to catch that when it happens and steer toward a more accepting and loving approach.

When you belong to yourself, it doesn't mean you are one hundred percent self-reliant and never need to consult anyone else for anything. It means you know how to trust your intuition, acknowledge your needs and emotions without shaming. It means that you will catch yourself, and accept yourself, when you stumble in life.

When everything you do has an underlying air of self-doubt, you may start to doubt whether you even belong in your own skin. You may operate in self-doubt unknowingly. Self-doubt is a practice that develops over time, through little actions of neglecting your own needs. Self-trust is also a practice that you can develop through little steps of learning to listen to yourself again.

Feeling like you truly belong somewhere is one of the greatest feelings we experience as humans. So, why wouldn't we hope to experience this within our own skin? What would it feel like to belong to yourself? What would it feel like to shift from self-doubt to undeniable trust that you have your own back? Believe it or not, you are capable of achieving this. Here are a few tangible ways you can work to build this feeling within yourself:

- **When making a big decision**, journal about your feelings toward the situation, and your preferred outcome.
- **When you feel uncomfortable socially**, stand up for yourself, or take a bathroom break to breathe and sort out your thoughts.
- **When you set a new goal**, focus on what feels doable and exciting for you personally.
- **When you fall short**, acknowledge your humanity. Practice forgiving yourself. Come up with a plan for how you can better support yourself and make sure you follow through next time.
- **When feeling a big emotion**, allow yourself to feel it fully. Journal, go for a walk with a friend, or find a way to process in the way that feels best for you.
- **When you notice negative thoughts,** work on steering back to an accepting and loving mindset. This does not mean forcing positivity. It simply means creating a supportive inner voice that feels accepting and trustworthy.

Through small gestures, you can slowly build self-trust. Explore which steps feel best for you and how you can begin implementing them into your life.

Acknowledge Your Strengths

Another great way to work on self-trust is by acknowledging your strengths. In which areas of life do you already trust yourself? Maybe you are great at your job and always deliver projects on time. Maybe you are a very loving and forgiving parent or friend. You could be a great driver, chef, gardener, partner, painter, cleaner, reader, or thinker. Take a second to think about the things you know you do well, no matter how big or small. Acknowledge that this is self-trust.

You are willing to admit that your strengths are your strengths because you trust yourself to do these things well. As humans, none of us do *everything* well, but we can always grow and develop new strengths. When we try new things, we don't know whether or not we will perform well. This uncertainty can fuel self-doubt if we let it. But what if you could somehow take the same trust you feel when performing your strengths, and apply it to areas of uncertainty?

Instead of trusting that you will succeed in every area of life, try trusting that you will *do your best*. And if your best does not meet your expectations, you can trust yourself to accept the humanity in that. Trust yourself to try again. Trust that each time, your best will get just a little bit better. This attitude will help you when setting goals. Instead of getting frustrated when you fall short, shaming yourself, thinking negative thoughts, and throwing in the towel, you can take a gentler approach. The approach of trying your best, acknowledging your humanity, and trying again tomorrow can be your new strength with a bit of practice.

Be Realistic and Follow Through

Through these efforts of exploring and practicing self-trust, it's important to be realistic with yourself. Don't set a goal of going to the gym five nights a week if you know you are busy six nights a week. You may be able to start small, build consistency, and eventually establish a routine of five workouts a week. That would be great! But the trick is to develop awareness surrounding your own needs, and develop realistic goals that reflect those needs. This shows your inner self they can trust you to set up a path for success.

Once you've established realistic goals, it's time to follow through. Following through is one of the important ways to develop self-trust. If your goal is to run twice a week, following through sends a message to your inner self that you are trustworthy. Every time you follow through, you strengthen this message, and the self-trust grows deeper. Of course, following through on goals, promises, or habits may not always be possible. Here is a simple guide for how to address these situations to maintain self-trust.

1. **Set a realistic goal.**
2. **Follow through.**
3. **Acknowledge slip-ups and adjust accordingly.**
4. **Establish a check-in, maybe weekly or monthly, to establish whether or not the goal**

is helping build self-trust.

5. **Repeat the tasks of following through and checking in repeatedly.**

Your path to cultivating self-trust will be unique to you, just like every other element of this process. Sit with what you have learned and take time to adjust it for your own needs. Taking what is helpful and tailoring it to align with your preferences is another step toward deepening your level of self-trust.

Week 5 Daily Affirmations

This week's affirmations focus on the concept of belonging to yourself, and learning to trust your decisions, intuition, and preferences. Use them as you explore self-trust in your daily activities. No matter your level of self-trust coming into this week, it's great to take a moment to acknowledge how you feel about this topic, and discover ways to strengthen the trust over time.

"I belong, fully and readily, to myself."

"I trust myself to set goals that are achievable for me."

"I keep the goals I set for myself."

"I trust myself completely, in every aspect of my life."

"I am getting to know myself, learning my strengths, and acknowledging my humanity."

"My self-trust is undeniable, and comes from a deep and honest place within."

"I am the one who makes the best decisions for me."

Week 5 Healing Activities

1. **Meditation:** Sit in a comfortable, upright position on the floor or in a chair. Lower your shoulders and release any tension in the face, jaw, and neck. Begin to breathe fully. When you exhale,

think the words, "I exhale self-doubt." When you inhale, think the words "I trust myself." Practice this deep breathing practice for two or three minutes, continuing to release doubts you feel about yourself on the exhale, and inhale trust and confidence. If you'd like, you can set a timer so that your full focus is on your breathing.

2. **Action Step**: Try to spend one day observing yourself and your levels of self-doubt. Jot down a short note each time you notice self-doubt arise. At the end of the day, observe your notes. Are there any patterns? Were you more doubtful of yourself around certain people, or in certain situations? Make a list of ways you can support yourself in these moments and try to implement them in the days to come.

3. **Self-hypnosis:** Read this script before you begin, making any adjustments you'd like to create a personal script for your recording. Once you've finished, record yourself saying the script slowly and clearly in an area with no background

noise. Pause for at least ten seconds after each line of text to give yourself time for visualization. Lie down in a comfortable position, relax your body, and replay the recording.

"Breathe in through your nose, and out through your mouth, quietly observing as your muscles slowly begin to relax.

Each time you exhale, your muscles relax further into the surface beneath you. You trust the surface to hold you and you relax completely. As your muscles relax more and more, your eyelids naturally grow heavy and begin to close.

You are now at the base of a mountain. You see the gorgeous, towering mountain stretch up above you. You see several paths before you. You select your preferred path and you take your first steps with ease and confidence.

You breathe in the mountain air as you make your way up the path. Each time you come across a forking path, you trust yourself to make the right decision and continue walking with endless confidence.

This ability to trust yourself gets easier and easier the higher up you get on the mountain. You know you are leading yourself in the exact direction you are supposed to go. You continue to breathe in self-trust, and breathe out confidence. You are fully relaxed and content with each step you take.

Now you are getting closer to the top of the mountain. You are flooded with a happy energy. You know that trusting yourself was the right decision. You reach a clearing, and the view at the top of the mountain is unbelievable.

You can see that your ability to make the right decisions for yourself led you here. This stunning view and this feeling of accomplishment show that trusting yourself was the best move. You see that trusting yourself is the easiest, most comforting thing you can do. You are growing more and more relaxed and comfortable with trusting your intuition.

You see that self trust is a beautiful, effortless thing. You can take time to assess, and make the decision to trust yourself with pure confidence.

Trust yourself now as you come back to awareness. Start to come back to consciousness by wiggling your fingers and toes. Open your eyes and carry the feeling you felt at the top of the mountain, the feeling of trust and joy, with you throughout your day."

Week 5 Reflection

1. Take some time to free-write your thoughts on how this week went. What did you enjoy? What was difficult? Which activities would you like to use again in the future?

2. Once you've reflected a bit about the week, come up with your own self-trust affirmation that sums up what you've learned. Try to pick a simple affirmation that can help you move past self-doubt and learn to trust your intuition.

Chapter 6

Protect Your Energy to Find Balance Between Rest and Activity

"Every person needs to take one day away. A day in which one consciously separates the past from the future. Jobs, family, employers, and friends can exist one day without any one of us, and if our egos permit us to confess, they could exist eternally in our absence. Each person deserves a day away in which no problems are confronted, no solutions searched for. Each of us needs to withdraw from the cares which will not withdraw from us."

Maya Angelou

(Wouldn't Take Nothing for My Journey Now, 1993)[7]

In today's fast-paced world, it's not hard to recall a time when you have denied yourself rest. Maybe there was a week where it felt like your to-do list was endless. You felt your eyes getting dry and heavy, your body slowing down, and your mind desperately trying to switch off. Maybe you have even had entire months or years that felt this way. In this situation, it's easy to think that resting would mean neglecting your responsibilities. However, you could also argue that *not* resting means neglecting your own needs.

When your body is tired, do you often push past the urge to rest in order to be more productive?

If you do allow yourself to rest, is that choice often paired with shame or guilt?

When you ignore your mental and physical needs, do you notice any patterns of fatigue, burn out, sickness, isolation, procrastination, or dread?

Life is stressful, and there are certainly moments when slowing down is not possible. I'm not saying drop everything and sleep for four months, although I am sure some of us could use that. I'm simply asking you to get curious. How often do you take stock of your mental and physical state? How often do you allow yourself to rest, completely free of guilt? How often do you shape your daily activities to be nurturing and informed by what is realistic for you? This week, let's consider the roles of rest and activity, and the importance of striking a balance between them. These building blocks are crucial to any self-love practice, so let's dive in and discover which self-loving steps are right for you.

Self-Neglect in Action

Do any bells go off for you when you hear the term self-neglect? Many people today neglect themselves by overworking and not checking in with their bodies and minds. This will eventually lead to burn out. Conversely, too much rest can also be a way of neglecting yourself. Maybe you have a big project due, and it becomes too overwhelming. You isolate yourself, stop spending time with friends, and stop doing the things you know you love because you don't feel you have "earned" them. When we neglect ourselves, we stop asking what our bodies need. We stop asking what our inner selves need. It is not a sustainable way to live, and eventually, our bodies will call this to our attention in one way or another.

Neglecting our needs makes us sick from the inside out. We procrastinate, we shame ourselves, and we repeat. Or we overwork, we get sick, and we repeat. These toxic behaviors corrode our self-worth because they are fueled by guilt. We are teaching our inner selves that they deserve to be punished either mentally or physically. So, how do we remove the guilt when it creeps into our behaviors like this? Here are a few ideas for restoring the balance between rest and activity in your life.

Behavior shift for self-loving rest:	Why it helps:	Example:
Practice compassion	If a child told you they were tired, you wouldn't force them to keep playing. If a friend said they needed to rest, you'd offer understanding and support. You deserve to treat yourself with that same compassion.	Your eyes get heavy after a long day of work. Instead of getting angry at your unfinished tasks, turn off your computer and say, "I did enough today. I am proud of my efforts. I grant myself permission to unwind."
Follow your intuition	Forcing more productivity when you're tired or checking out when you're overwhelmed both shut off your connection to your intuition. Start listening to your gut when you need rest, so you can restore and bounce back faster.	You are at work but find your mind constantly wandering from your current task. Instead of getting frustrated but continuing to procrastinate, try taking an intentional ten-minute break. Let your mind settle before returning to the task.

Build in breaks	Endless streaks of productivity are not natural for the human brain. We need a mix of action and rest, and a healthy variety in our daily activities. Building in breaks will help you see rest as a crucial part of your daily routine instead of something to be ashamed of.	Write one or two ten-minute breaks into your day whenever possible. You can set an alarm or write them into your calendar. Make a point to move your body and get a change of scenery during this time. Consider these plans just as important as your other daily tasks.
Rest IS the activity	Instead of "resting" while talking on the phone, writing an email, or doing another work task, see rest as the activity. Cutting out the urge to multitask will ensure you get full enjoyment out of your restful efforts.	When you rest, avoid using a phone, computer, or any other device that puts your mind elsewhere. Try to use the time to check in with your mind and body and acknowledge that you deserve this time to restore.

As simple as it sounds, the key to this process is remembering that you are human. You are not a machine. You are only capable of so much, and no amount of guilt will magically bring you an endless supply of time and energy. So why not offer yourself a bit of kindness instead? Why not work to transform your relationship with rest? After all, mending this relationship has the potential to transform the rest of your life.

Rest to Transform

What I'm getting at here is the fact that we put a lot of energy into resisting rest, shaming ourselves for needing rest, and mentally checking out rather than giving in to rest. But maybe, just maybe, removing this resistance and mental chatter will prove more helpful. Reclaiming your relationship to rest has the potential to drastically improve your life. Here are a few areas this effort will help transform:

- **Your ability to set and keep boundaries**

- **The quality of your time spent in reflection**
- **Your decision-making skills**
- **Your levels of self-acceptance and self-worth**
- **Your ability to trust yourself**
- **Your ability to heal pain that you have stored in your body**
- **The quality of your inner dialogue**
- **Your productivity**
- **Your level of efficiency**
- **The amount of joy you get out of both rest and activity**

Learning to enjoy rest and make time for it helps mend your relationship with your inner self. You tell that version of you that you are worth more than your level of productivity. Each time you send this message, you strengthen the impact it has. Any good leader knows that showing kindness and understanding will boost the productivity of their team. When people feel heard, and when their needs feel honored, they show up more fully in their roles. They get more done and feel more satisfied at the end of the day. Do you think you could be your own leader in this area? Could you try putting your wellbeing first, just to see what happens?

Finding Ease in Your Activities

We've established that removing shame will establish a more self-loving approach to rest. So, what if we apply the same idea to our activities in life? Many of us take on too much in our roles at work. We push ourselves to accomplish more, faster. Sometimes we even do this with our weekends and free time. We pack all of our downtime with activities to try and make the most of each moment. However, even the activities we enjoy the most, if done in an effort to pressure ourselves, become just another means of self-punishment.

Think about it. Have you ever had a few days off work, and just wanted to spend them resting, watching movies, and maybe going on a few long walks? Maybe the pressure of needing to make the most of the time got the best of you, and you booked a trip to a nearby town. You packed the days full of activities and returned to work feeling just as exhausted as ever. Now, maybe an action-packed trip is your idea of relaxation. Everyone is different. The question is, when you have free time, what is the guiding force in how you decide to spend that time? Is it a gentle, kind, curious approach to meeting your own needs? Is it a mix of guilt, anxiety, and fear of missing out? Is this guiding force similar to the one that guides your efforts at work, and your decisions to rest?

Self-love is all about getting to the root of these questions and starting to work in alignment with your own needs. If you need rest, carve out time for a nice bubble bath or cozy movie on the sofa. If you need some activity to disconnect, plan a hike or a day-trip with friends. Even just taking five minutes to breathe and release muscle tension during your workday can be a big step. Get curious about your needs. Let what you discover steer you toward a few self-loving steps today. Repeat tomorrow.

Week 6 Daily Affirmations

This week's affirmations focus on healing your

relationship with rest. You're encouraged to check in with your mental and physical needs and make compassionate decisions for yourself. Use these affirmations if you feel any resistance toward resting. Get curious about this aspect of your mental dialogue, and be patient as you steer toward a more self-loving approach to thinking about rest.

"I did enough today. I am proud of my efforts. I grant myself permission to unwind."

"I allow myself to rest fully, completely free of worries."

"I choose daily activities based on my personal preferences and needs."

"I operate in communion with my inner self. I am my own best guiding force."

"I notice resistance to rest and let it pass. I choose to care for myself now."

"I am healing my mindset regarding work and rest. I work hard and feel proud. I rest hard and feel proud."

"I vow to check in with my mental and physical needs and honor them. I am building this practice from a place of deep self-respect."

Week 6 Healing Activities

1. **Check-in meditation:** Lay down on a comfortable, flat surface, and close your eyes. Begin to breathe fully in through your nose, and out through your mouth. First, allow your focus to come to your feet. Notice your toes, arches, and ankles. Thank your feet for everything they do for you, and allow them to relax completely. Repeat this process of noticing, thanking, and releasing with your calves, then knees, then thighs. As you work your way up your body, continue checking in and allowing your body to relax more and more. Once you reach the top of your head, allow a feeling of peace to come over

you. Sit in this feeling as long as you like, knowing both your body and mind deserve to relax this deeply.

2. **Action Step**: Take a moment during or after your workday to give yourself a hand massage. Remove any jewelry, use a lotion or oil if that feels nice, and gently massage your hands. Start with the palms and work your way up to the soft skin between each finger. Breathe in and out and let the other muscle tension in your body begin to melt away. Massage all the way to the end of each finger, one at a time. Use this as an opportunity to notice the work your hands do for you each day, how they feel, and how they deserve this moment of rest.

3. **Restful Self-hypnosis:** Read this script before you begin, making any adjustments you'd like to create a personal script for your recording. Once you've finished, record yourself saying the script slowly and clearly in an area with no background noise. Pause for at least ten seconds after each

line of text to give yourself time for visualization. Lie down in a comfortable position, relax your body, and replay the recording.

"Breathe in through your nose and out through your mouth, allowing your face to relax. Continue breathing as you observe your neck muscles and shoulders softening into a restful state.

As you breathe in, you imagine a profound heaviness drifting over your body. When you breathe out, you surrender completely to a restful bliss.

You are surrounded by the most comforting blankets and pillows. You feel warm, safe, and completely relaxed. You know you deserve rest, and you receive it with ease now.

Your breath grows slower and slower. You are surrounded by infinite comforts. You accept the warmth and security you feel as you drift down deeper into a more restful state.

You recognize that letting go and allowing rest to take over is so restorative, here in this deep, relaxed state. You know you are free to access this deep rest at any moment you choose.

You are still drifting down into the sea of cozy blankets and pillows. You feel complete bliss. You know that rest will take over if you just let go. You are learning to let go and trust that you deserve this serene and blissful relaxation. Everything else falls away and you fall into an effortless restful state.

You know that you can and should achieve this deep state of rest every day. This comfortable, infinite, blissful state is yours whenever you want it.

You are building a beautiful balance between activity and rest. You can call upon this restful state with ease. Every night, you fall into this luxurious comfort, and you wake up completely restored.

Start to come back to consciousness by wiggling your fingers and toes. Gently open your eyes and maintain this restful quality in your body and mind. Continue to bring this feeling with you into your other restful activities."

Week 6 Reflection

1. Take some time to free-write your thoughts on how this week went. What did you enjoy? What was difficult? Which activities would you like to use again in the future?

2. Once you've reflected a bit about the week, come up with your own affirmation that sums up what you've learned about the importance of rest. Try to pick a simple affirmation that can help you ease any resistance you feel toward resting your body and mind.

Chapter 7

Create an Inner Voice of Kindness and Compassion

"Remember, you have been criticizing yourself for years and it hasn't worked. Try approving of yourself and see what happens."

Louise Hay (*You Can Heal Your Life*, 1984)[8]

Last week, we discussed the importance of adjusting your inner dialogue surrounding rest. Now, let's take that concept a bit further. What would it be like to have an inner voice that offered kindness before criticism, compassion before shame?

Say you want to ask for a raise at work. You've spent years going above and beyond, and seen many coworkers get raises since you started your job. You've thought of every variable, spoken with your peers, and logically you know you have every right to ask for an increase in salary. But, there is a voice in your head telling you that you're an imposter. The voice says you don't really deserve the raise, or maybe you don't even deserve the job at all. Despite the heaps of evidence that this voice is incorrect, it has still kept you from mustering the courage to ask for the raise.

Do you let the voice in your head convince you to settle for less than you deserve?

Do you find that your thoughts tend to be critical or doubtful rather than encouraging or kind?

Do you get caught up believing your negative thoughts to be true? Do you think this could be holding you back in more than one area of your life?

Many of us tend to have naturally negative inner dialogues. We are critical when we look in the mirror, make mistakes at work, or say the wrong thing in front of friends. We doubt our worth in relationships, and if we receive negative treatment, we may come up with reasons that we deserved to be treated poorly. When we experience the inevitable negativity of life, we feel discomfort or pain, and we are often our own easiest target to blame for the discomfort we feel. However, beating ourselves up through negative self-talk only exacerbates this pain.

Of course, pain is an inevitable part of life, which can be infuriating to accept. However, if this is the case, why are we so willing to increase the pain with a critical inner voice? Wouldn't it be a relief to turn inward and find kindness there instead? Wouldn't creating a compassionate inner voice be the ultimate act of self-love?

Make Peace With Your Inner Voice

Let's take a minute here to remember that we are not looking to critique our current selves. Our inner voices likely do enough of that already. Before you make any shifts or adjustments, try to make peace with the current state of your inner dialogue.

Take a few breaths to sit and observe your thoughts now. Do you notice any judgment, resistance, or urges to critique yourself or this process? Do you notice a desire for quick and easy change, to "fix" yourself, or skip ahead to get to the "real progress?" This is all your inner dialogue trying to convince you that you should be somewhere, anywhere, other than where you are. Ultimately, this is a way of resisting the feelings you are currently feeling, and denying your inner self the compassion needed to heal and grow.

Whatever you are feeling right now, and however your inner dialogue is treating you, know this. Your inner voice developed as a way to cope with your unique circumstances. It is another normal side-effect of being human. It can be molded and sculpted to better serve you as you move toward a more self-loving path. Accepting where you are now is the first and most crucial step toward creating this shift. Here are a few ways you can work to make peace with your inner voice:

Inner-Self Peace Offering Suggestions:
Take a moment to sit with your eyes closed and observe your thoughts. Acknowledge when they are positive and when they are negative. When they are negative, think the words, "I forgive you." When they are positive, think the words, "thank you."
Practice noticing when you are caught in self-critical thinking. Instead of continuing down that rabbit hole, invite yourself out for a walk instead.
Journal about the ways your negative inner dialogue has limited you or hurt you in the past. When you are done, write the words, "I accept this tendency as a part of who I am. I love myself as I am, and I am ready to shift to a more loving inner voice."

Little by little, you will start to believe these kind gestures and accept them. Continue practicing acceptance of who you are NOW, no matter how frustrated you get with yourself and the negative thoughts that creep back in. Stay curious and patient with yourself. Creating a peace offering, and repeatedly showing your inner self that you accept them for who they are, will slowly create the shift you are looking for. In this case, making peace does not mean remaining unchanged, because making peace is likely a new act for you. It's a vow to end the internal fight, letting your outer and inner selves work together, maybe for the first time. Stick with this, and you will begin to notice a shift toward a more forgiving and compassionate inner voice.

Shifting Toward Compassion

We may be more likely to critique the feminine parts of ourselves. This could be due to dynamics in childhood or ideas ingrained in us by society. There are plenty of outside forces that say certain parts of ourselves are simply "too much." After a while, we start to believe them, and attempt to shrink these parts of ourselves. Here are a few examples of feminine characteristics, those soft, intuitive, nurturing sides of ourselves, and how willing we are to view them as negative. I'll also include ways we can shift toward compassion by beginning to see these characteristics as vital parts of the whole.

Feminine quality:	We critique this quality as:	We can reclaim this quality by:
A desire for connection	Being too needy, clingy, or desperate for attention	Recognizing that human connection is vital, and we deserve to communicate our need for it without feeling judgment or shame.
Self-expression	Being too dramatic, stubborn, emotional, silly, annoying, or childish	Recognizing that creativity, play, and expression are fundamental elements of life. They help us learn, grow, and heal.
Intuition	Jumping to conclusions, being irrational, or being impulsive	Building self-trust, learning to acknowledge our inner voice, and making decisions that feel nurturing

Empathy	Being too sensitive, too serious, or being a people-pleaser	Acknowledging that empathy enriches our relationships when we maintain healthy boundaries surrounding our needs
Sensitivity	Being weak, too uptight, or too intense	Seeing sensitivity as an ability to feel everything life has to offer more fully; Taking emotional overwhelm as a cue to slow down and gain clarity
Generosity	Being a pleaser, over-sharing, giving too many chances, or not having strong boundaries	Maintaining healthy boundaries, and seeing generosity as a gift to those we love, as long as we are also offering it to ourselves

These are just a few examples of qualities you may see as "difficult to love" within yourself. When you view yourself as "too much," it becomes easy to dismiss your own needs, abandon your inner self, and avoid healing the pain you feel. As much as it may seem challenging to embrace certain aspects of who you are, sitting with the discomfort is a compassionate first step. Being willing to even acknowledge these characteristics is a sign that you are making a necessary internal shift toward kindness. Slowly, this compassionate inner voice will grow. Eventually, you'll recognize that carrying compassion with you makes life's difficult moments a bit less harsh. Maybe it will even make the good times a bit sweeter too.

Build a Flow of Kindness

That's the point in all of this. If you create a compassionate inner dialogue, one that reaches for kindness before criticism, you create a tool you can draw upon at any moment. It's an inner support system that helps you through hardship and celebrates your successes. You do this one moment at a time. You do this by journaling, taking time for a favorite hobby, going on a long hike, meditating, preparing a delicious meal for yourself, or however you prefer to check in. Check in, notice the quality of your thoughts, replace anything negative with a compassionate thought like, "You are doing your best, and that is good enough." Over time, these small steps build up and expand out into other areas of your life.

Maybe building a flow of inner kindness is the peace offering you've always needed. Maybe it still feels foreign and uncomfortable. Either way, lean in just to notice how you feel. Remember, before anything you read or attempt in this book, always consider your needs first. What would be the kindest gesture you could offer yourself right now?

Week 7 Daily Affirmations

This week's affirmations focus on that act of making a peace offering to your inner self. Use them to help you train your mind to shift out of judgment and into a place of kindness and compassion. Stay patient and know that no matter where you are in the process, you are building a loving support system within yourself.

"I am at peace with my inner voice. It protects me and showers me with love in each moment, and I am grateful."

"My truest self dwells within me. I offer this self persistent love and trust."

"Each time my inner dialogue becomes critical, I effortlessly shift toward a mindset of compassion."

"Kindness flows within me and expands out into every connection in my life."

"I see my inner self as a friend. I choose to make peace with every version of myself."

"I deserve to feel joy, regardless of my shortcomings. I deserve love, even if there are parts of myself I am still learning to love well."

"My inner world is a safe place for me to reside. I feel calm and at peace with myself."

Week 7 Healing Activities

1. **Kindness Meditation:** Sit down on a

comfortable, flat surface, and close your eyes. Begin to breathe fully in through your nose, and out through your mouth. Clasp your hands together gently and place them in your lap. Notice how it feels to hold your own hand. Notice any resistance you feel to this simple gesture. Continue to notice your breaths in and out. Think the words, "I am here for you." Imagine your clasped hands represent the connection of your inner and outer selves. Continue to sit in stillness, offering your inner self a moment of kindness for at least three minutes. Notice how this offering feels in your body.

2. **Action Step**: Write a few "kindness notes" for yourself, and stick them around your house. You can use the affirmations for this week, or create your own messages you think would lift your spirits throughout the day. Put them on your bathroom mirror, refrigerator, steering wheel, desk at work, or anywhere else you will see them often. Notice how these little gestures of kindness impact your mood.

3. **Peace Offering Self-hypnosis:** Read this script before you begin, making any adjustments you'd like to create a personal script for your recording. Once you've finished, record yourself saying the script slowly and clearly in an area with no background noise. Pause for at least ten seconds after each line of text to give yourself time for visualization. Lie down in a comfortable position, relax your body, and replay the recording.

"Take a deep breath and allow your hands to clasp together gently. Exhale and feel the warmth your hands begin to generate as they relax together.

As you breathe in, imagine you are sitting across from your inner self. Your inner self bows to you and you bow to them. You grow more and more relaxed as you accept the peace that is growing within you.

As your outer self and inner self radiate compassionate, kind energy between them, you begin to notice a warmth surrounding you.

This warmth is as powerful and bright as the sun. It embraces you fully. The kindness expressed within yourself has woken up more inner selves that are radiating acceptance and love.

You know that these selves represent you at each moment of your life, past, present, and future. You recognize that they are each offering unwavering kindness and compassion to you now.

The warmth expands out infinitely, and each of the infinite selves are embraced by its light. You know that these selves have infinite love and acceptance for you. You know that you can always turn inward and find their kindness radiating toward you.

You can access this inner compassion in any given moment. It joins you wherever you go, and you can tap into it as readily as feeling the warmth of the sun on your skin.

You are tapping into your own endlessly kind and compassionate inner voice. This voice is growing stronger and more confident in each moment. Each time you feel warmth you are reminded of this compassionate love inside of you.

Bring this warmth with you as you return back to consciousness. Wiggle your fingers and toes and slowly open your eyes. Tap into this kind and compassionate inner voice to make peace with yourself throughout the day."

Week 7 Reflection

1. Take some time to free-write your thoughts on how this week went. What did you enjoy? What was difficult? Which activities would you like to use again in the future?
2. Once you've reflected a bit about the week, come up with your own affirmation that sums up what you've learned about creating a compassionate inner voice. Try to pick a simple affirmation that can help you shift away from critical thinking and toward a place of kindness.

DID YOU ENJOY THIS BOOK?

We would truly appreciate if you could leave a review on Amazon. We are an independent publishing company and read each and every review!

Chapter 8

Build a Self-Image of Strength and Resilience

"And one has to understand that braveness is not the absence of fear but rather the strength to keep on going forward despite the fear."

Paulo Coelho (Goodreads, 2014)[9]

Think back to the last time you tried learning a new skill. Maybe this was something recent, or maybe your experiences in childhood come to mind, like learning to swim or ride a bicycle. You were starting from scratch, but you were likely hopeful that you would eventually master the skill. However, after hours of practice, trying and failing, falling and getting back up again, you started to feel like giving up. Whether you had someone helping you or you were learning on your own, someone had to convince you to persevere. That voice that told you not to give up, the voice that had faith in you despite your fears and struggles, is the reason that you kept going and eventually learned the skill.

Do you notice a tendency to want to give up when things are difficult?

Do you lose faith in yourself quickly, or have you learned to override thoughts that tell you you will not succeed?

If you have a sense of determination or faith in

yourself to succeed, what does that feel like? Does it feel like confidence, or does it feel like shaming yourself into performing at your best?

We all have some version of a self-image. This is as literal as what you see when you look in the mirror. It is also how you predict you will behave in certain situations, like how you think you will perform at work or when trying something new. Often, this self-image does play a role in predicting how we will perform. If the way we view ourselves is limiting, like not expecting ourselves to perform well under stress, we increase the likelihood that this prediction will come true. We can take a self-loving route by deciding to expand our self-image, to have a bit more confidence in the person we see in the mirror. When we create a self-image that incorporates confidence, strength, and resilience, we take a big step toward removing our inner roadblocks and opening up new doors for ourselves.

What is Your Self-Image?

We can have a self-image related to many different areas of life. Over time we develop a sense of what kind of friend, parent, sibling, partner, or worker we are. These images may be different relative to the area of life they encompass, but they likely have overarching similarities. If we have a generally positive view of ourselves, our self-image will likely be more positive. A negative inner dialogue may lend itself to a more negative self-image. We get so used to these ways that we view ourselves that we may not even notice them anymore. We begin to see this perception of ourselves as an undeniable truth. However, it may be beneficial to notice this tendency and get curious about where these thoughts are coming from. Let's take a look at a few questions you can ask yourself about your self-image.

Example of Self-Image Mistaken for Truth:	Non-judgmental Question for Getting Curious About this Thought:
"I am shy and lack confidence in social situations."	Is my shyness or lack of confidence really an effort to avoid putting myself out there?
"I procrastinate and tend to be lazy at work."	Is the thought that I am a procrastinator the reason I give in to procrastination? Do I procrastinate because I need more of a challenge, or because I have a fear that I will not succeed?
"When trying new things, I become frustrated quickly and give up easily."	Is my frustration because I feel that I am not good enough? If I viewed myself as good enough, would I be more willing to stick with difficult tasks?
"I am sensitive and defensive when receiving criticism."	Is my sensitivity rooted in the thought that criticism indicates that I am not worthy or capable?

"I am not feminine/ fashionable/ put-together/ attractive enough."	Whose standard am I judging myself by? Maybe embracing my body and my preferences regarding physical appearance would be a more loving approach?
"I cannot thrive in high-stress situations."	Are specific situations overwhelming to me because of the pressure I place on myself, or a lack of confidence in myself to succeed? Could I set up boundaries to take care of myself first, even in stressful situations?

Just like everything else we have discussed so far, your self-image is a natural product of your experiences in life and how you have responded to them. Every life experience, no matter how big or small, has been integrated into the perception you have of yourself. It is important to recognize a few things here. This is natural and happens to each of us. However, depending on a variety of factors, your self-image may not accurately represent who you are. If you mistake it for the truth, you place a number of limitations on how you operate in the world, and what you perceive yourself to be capable of. Recognizing this, you can begin shifting your self-image to a more positive place. You can realize that you already have more resilience and strength than you think. Not only will this shift your thinking process and expand your view of the possibilities in your life. It will also help you to worry less about the perceptions you believe other people have of you.

Restore Connections by Finding an Inner Friend

When we have negative thoughts about ourselves, we tend to expand them outward. We try to guess what other people think about us, and usually decide that their thoughts of us are also negative. Our self-image has this power to spread outside of ourselves and impact how we relate to the people around us. Here are a few ways negative self-image impacts our connections with the people in our lives:

- **We judge other people for the same reasons we judge ourselves.**
- **We gossip about other people to distract from our own insecurities.**
- **We assume everyone is judging and gossiping about us as well.**
- **We assume everyone's view of us is an exact replica of the negative ways we view ourselves.**
- **Interactions become defensive or distorted when we assume others see the worst in us.**
- **When we project our thoughts onto another person, we lose the ability to connect with them and really hear what they are saying.**

Do you see how clinging hard to a negative self-image can disrupt your connections with others? Unless we are judging others for the same reasons we judge ourselves, we often offer the people in our lives much more gentleness and grace than we give ourselves. Either way, this is an act of viewing ourselves as inferior to those around us. We forgive friends for their mistakes and understand when they are having an off day. We sit with them, give them a pep talk, and help them get to feeling better again. What would it be like if we offered this type of friendship to ourselves as well? What would it be like to see ourselves as just as deserving of kindness as the people we care about?

Viewing yourself as a friend reminds you to see the humanness in yourself again. It reminds you that an off day, a perceived weakness, or even a failure should not diminish the love you extend to yourself. Instead of attacking yourself and allowing your self-image to become more and more negative, you can offer yourself a pep talk. You can recognize that mistakes and fears are a part of life, and we don't need to read too much into them. Over time, this offering of friendship will help you remember your strength and bounce back quicker after setbacks.

The Courage to Rewrite Your Self-Image

Resilience is such an integral part of the human condition. When we fall, we get back up. Our bodies even know how to heal the scrapes and bruises we get along the way. If our bodies are such experts at healing wounds, do you think our minds are capable of a similar type of restoration?

The human mind is certainly complicated, but we do not have to be victims of the thinking styles that we have developed over time. If you view yourself in a negative light, or are hyper-critical when you make mistakes, know that you have the power to rewrite this tendency. These shifts take a bit of effort, and it may be useful to have a qualified professional help you get there. But even giving yourself this time to explore the ways you view yourself takes courage. Observing your own self-image, and acknowledging your power to build a new one, is a loving first step forward.

Take some time to think about what you want your self-image to be. Even if you don't believe these things about yourself just yet, exploring how you'd like to view yourself can provide great information as you work to rewrite your perception of yourself. Here are a few ideas for how you may want to view yourself. Create your own list, writing a few of these in a journal, or adding your own self-image goals:

Examples of Self-Image Goals:
"I am strong. I can handle criticism, stress, and hardship without questioning my own strength."
"I am confident in all social situations. I look after myself rather than attempting to please others."
"My sensitivity is an asset. My emotions are indicators of my needs. They help me connect more fully to myself and others."
"I can thrive in any situation I am faced with. If I find that I am struggling to thrive, I will protect myself rather than shaming myself."
"I am a hard worker, and I no longer allow fear or self-doubt to affect my performance."

Here's the thing. You deserve a self-image that creates possibilities rather than limitations. You deserve an inner space that is curious and friendly, and acknowledges the strength you already possess. You've made it to the end of chapter 8, so allow yourself to see the courage it has taken to stick with this process. The fact that you are here is indicative of the fact that you are beginning to see your worth. Whether or not you have fully embraced it, you are beginning to offer yourself genuine love. That alone is worth celebrating.

Week 8 Daily Affirmations

The affirmations for this week encourage you to acknowledge your internal strength and resilience. Use them as a focal point as you move toward a more positive self-image. Keeping these ideas in mind will remind you to be gentle and treat yourself as you would a friend. This offering of softness, kindness, and friendship will build a foundation for rewriting a positive and unwavering self-image of strength.

"I let criticism slide off my back. No one's opinion can change the love I feel for myself."

"Being human, making mistakes, and showing up again anyway is the ultimate act of courage."

"I trust myself to handle anything that comes my way with resilience and grace."

"I see myself as a sturdy force of love and strength."

"As I reveal my softness, my vulnerability, and my fears, I show up as my strongest self."

"There are lessons in both failure and success. Neither outcome affects my self-image because it is solid and unwavering."

"When I look in the mirror, I see someone who is trying to be better to themselves. I see that as the ultimate act of strength."

Week 8 Healing Activities

1. **Expansive Self-Image Meditation:** Sit down on a comfortable, flat surface and close your eyes. Begin to breathe fully in through your nose, and out through your mouth. Imagine there is a golden light surrounding you. As you breathe in, the light glows brighter. As you breathe out, it expands. You watch the light continue to expand and grow past the room you are in. It gets bigger and bigger until it is the size of your house, and then the size of your town, and then the size of your country. Soon, this light is bigger than the Earth itself. From your new perspective, everything in your life is small, and nothing can impact the size and the brightness of this light you have created. Continue to breathe in and out, noticing how it feels to have created such expansive energy, knowing that nothing can diminish it.

2. **Self-Image Goals Action Step**: Earlier in the chapter, you may have created a list of your self-image goals. If so, pull it out now. Choose one of the ways you wish to view yourself, and spend one day trying to embody this image. Notice the ways you embody this image with ease. Notice the moments that it is more difficult to continue embodying the image. If you want more confidence, maybe it is easy to be confident when walking down the street, but more difficult when you are chatting with your boss. Just notice these moments without judgment and write them down. This information will help you learn which types of situations affect your self-image the most. From there you can brainstorm ways to work toward maintaining a positive self-image, even when faced with difficult situations.

3. **Strong Self-Image Self-hypnosis:** Read this script before you begin, making any adjustments you'd like to create a personal script for your

recording. Once you've finished, record yourself saying the script slowly and clearly in an area with no background noise. Pause for at least ten seconds after each line of text to give yourself time for visualization. Lie down in a comfortable position, relax your body, and replay the recording.

"Breathe in and out, allowing a vibrant energy to wash over your body. You see this energy as strength and resilience, and accept them with ease as you settle in.

Breathe in, allowing this strength to wash over you. Breathe out, relaxing into the surface beneath you. You accept this vibrant energy, and allow it to calm you as you relax deeper.

You see your connection with the surface beneath you as the roots of a tree. They are growing deep down into the Earth now. They are solid and growing stronger with each breath. The energy and strength you feel effortlessly expand down into your roots, reaching deeper into the layers of the Earth.

Your body feels so relaxed and content now as you watch yourself sprout up like a tree. Your trunk thickens and grows taller and taller. You expand to take up more and more space, towering over the world around you.

You feel the strength you have inside of you emanating outward. This is an effortless sensation and it feels glorious.

You see yourself as this powerful, towering tree now. You know this unwavering strength is inside of you. You know you are a resilient being. This is the self-image you choose to see for yourself now.

You can access this sensation at any time. The deep, powerful roots, and the beautiful, towering strength are very much part of who you are. This is what you choose to see when you look in the mirror now.

This strong and resilient self-image is becoming easier and easier for you to tap into. You are doing such a good job of seeing yourself in this incredible new way. You are shifting your self-image so effortlessly now.

Let this vibrant energy trickle into your awareness as you slowly wiggle your fingers and toes. Open your eyes and carry this feeling with you as you stand up and continue your day."

Week 8 Reflection

1. Take some time to free-write your thoughts on how this week went. What did you enjoy? What was difficult? Which activities would you like to use again in the future?

2. Once you've reflected a bit about the week, come up with your own self-image affirmation that sums up what you've learned. Try to pick a simple affirmation that will offer gentleness and grace, while also helping you view yourself as strong.

Chapter 9

Celebrate Your Efforts and Bask in the Small Successes

"The journey of a thousand miles begins with a single step."

Lao Tzu (Goodreads, 2020)[10]

By now, you know that self-love isn't only found in the grand gestures in life. There is plenty of self-love to be found in ordinary, everyday tasks. Say you have needed a car wash for months. You keep putting it off because tasks at work, chores at home, and family activities continue to get in the way. This small task that will mostly only benefit you gets put on the back burner. Before you know it, it has been six months since you first realized you needed a car wash.

Are there any simple, mundane tasks in your life that you tend to put off?

If you know you feel so much better when these simple tasks are done, why do you put them off?

If you let yourself feel shame or guilt for not doing these things, do you also allow yourself to celebrate once you have gotten them done?

These little things like getting a car wash, trimming your

nails, or clearing out the junk drawer may seem unimportant, but they can have a big impact on how we view ourselves and our lives. Putting the things off that you know you need to do, especially when you are the main person who will benefit from the task being done, can begin to feel like self-neglect. The reminder that you still haven't done the task, like seeing your dirty car in the garage every day, sends a small dose of shame to your inner self. When we look at it this way, we can start to see that these tiny efforts do matter. They serve as a reminder that we aren't putting our own needs last anymore. As simple as it seems to clean out a junk drawer, it is also an act of self-love worthy of celebrating!

True Self-Celebration

There is great importance in celebrating yourself, your skills, your efforts, and even the smallest victories. When we reserve celebration for the big accomplishments, we send the message to ourselves that those are the only times worth celebrating.

Learning to celebrate the little things in life can play a crucial role in developing self-love.

Instead of hustling day after day, and only patting yourself on the back after a big achievement, why not build a bit of celebration into each day? Taking the time to appreciate yourself for the little things injects a bit of self-love into the ordinary tasks of our daily lives. Here are a few ideas for what celebrating yourself could look like:

Everyday Task You Normally Wouldn't Celebrate:	Idea for Celebrating this Simple Accomplishment:
You finally got a car wash.	Pick up a friend and go on a nice, long drive to catch up.
You cooked yourself a healthy meal.	Go on a stroll around the block to unwind and appreciate your body.

You cleaned out your junk drawer.	Add a bit of happiness to the space, like a photo of you and your family or a nice hand-written affirmation, to celebrate your organization and encourage you to keep it that way.
You did your taxes.	Create a gratitude journal to remind yourself of the good things that happened, even on stressful days.
You sat through a long, dull meeting at work.	Take a break before jumping back into work by doing some stretches, playing a round of ping pong, or going for a walk.

You don't have to throw yourself a party every time you do the dishes. These efforts of celebrating yourself can be as small as thinking one nice thought. We might normally tend to shame ourselves into a task like doing the dishes by thinking, "My house is a mess. I can't believe I let it get this bad!" Shifting this thought to, "I am doing the best I can, and I appreciate my effort to make my home a more comfortable place to be," turns the thought into an act of celebration. This kindness will make us a bit more optimistic about the monotonous tasks in life. We may even begin to get more joy out of ordinary things, rather than reserving our joy for the infrequent occurrence of a "big accomplishment."

The Little Things Are the Big Things

The sheer fact that there are so many small, seemingly insignificant tasks in life is reason enough to consider celebrating them. Each second passes by so quickly, but in the end, these seconds come together to create our memories and our life's story. Here are a few ways that celebrating the small moments in life can have a big impact:

- **Cultivate more presence during the ordinary activities in life.**
- **Observe your thoughts and begin to treat yourself better when completing simple tasks.**

- **Learn what motivates you and apply the knowledge to increase your productivity.**
- **Move past limitations more easily and get tasks accomplished faster.**
- **Remove shame and guilt as primary motivators.**
- **Stop sabotaging your own daily routines by building a small reward into unpleasant activities.**
- **Add more joy, humor, and excitement into boring or stressful situations.**
- **Stop letting your negative thoughts impede your enjoyment throughout the day.**
- **Be gentle with yourself when you make mistakes or struggle to finish a task.**
- **Bounce back faster when you do encounter hurdles.**

Getting more out of the little things will help you get more joy out of life. A little more joy, more satisfaction, more presence, and more authenticity will add up quickly. Life is a collection of billions of tiny, often boring, seemingly meaningless moments. Wouldn't celebrating these moments be another meaningful offering of self-love?

Make it a Habit!

Just like the other self-love practices we've discussed, self-celebration may not come naturally at first. When you are used to punishing and shaming yourself through your daily activities, you may need frequent reminders to shift into a positive mindset and stay there. But with patience, time, and persistence, celebrating yourself and finding joy in the little moments can become your new normal. Just as you developed your current coping strategies for getting through the monotonous moments of the day, you can work to develop new strategies that serve you better.

First, you'll want to figure out what motivates you. Do you get enjoyment out of catching up with friends, a physical activity, spending time alone journaling or meditating, or planning your next road trip? Learn your positive motivators and turn them into small moments of celebration throughout the day.

Next, you'll want to make a list of the celebration strategies you plan to use, and set reminders to act on them during the day. These activities should be very small, so they don't feel like another item on the to-do list. These may even be activities you would do during the day anyway, as a method of procrastination. Being intentional with these activities can help you eliminate that procrastination by consciously building celebration moments into your day. Here are some examples of how this could look:

Everyday Task:	Preferred Activity:	Incorporating an Intentional Celebration Habit:
Working on a tedious data-entry project at work	Doing yoga	Set an alarm for one hour of work. Once you've finished the hour, take a break to do some stretches!

Cleaning the floors in your house	Catching up with friends	When you've cleaned half of the floors, take a break to send a friend a voice message or text to catch up!
Organizing your home	Going for a walk	After completing a chunk of the organization, or finishing one task, go for a short walk to clear your mind before continuing with other tasks!
Waiting on the phone with customer service	Planning a trip	While waiting on the phone, make a list of places you want to go or things you need to do to plan the trip. After you've finished the call, celebrate by completing one task on the trip to-do list!

Of course, these habits will look different for everyone. The important thing is exploring which tasks you dread, and which you love, and realize that you can use this information to your advantage! Instead of working against yourself by procrastinating, and shaming yourself for procrastination, you can learn to power through the dull moments and reward yourself with the activities you love! This is a simple yet important way that you can start working in communion with your own needs. Learn that you deserve to set aside time to celebrate yourself every day. Making this a habit is another powerful act of self-love.

Small Steps, Big Impact

By now, I hope you've realized that the time to celebrate is now. You are almost at the finish line of this self-love exploration, but the journey doesn't end here. The small steps and tiny adjustments you have made over the past nine weeks have come together to mean much more. You've gotten curious, stayed patient, and observed the steps that work best for you. You've stuck with this journey when you were met with difficulty, discomfort, and resistance. You may still feel far away from the idea of self-love, but the steps you've taken have all been loving. This is where you come to embody self-love. This is why small, persistent, daily steps are so worth celebrating. When we see the tiny moments of our lives as valuable, we realize that it is in these moments that we can heal, grow, and practice treating ourselves a bit kinder.

Week 9 Daily Affirmations

This week's affirmations focus on the act of caring for and appreciating yourself in each moment. The act of celebrating yourself reminds you that you have your own back no matter what. Whether you are working on an important project or simply doing the dishes, celebrating yourself adds moments of awareness and self-love into your day. Use these affirmations to remind yourself that celebration should not just be reserved for big achievements. Instead, celebrate the ordinary, and watch how this transforms your days.

"I am learning to notice the moments when I choose to take care of myself."

"I celebrate the little things. I am always looking out for me."

"I celebrate myself every day."

"My true self is showing up more and more every day."

"My habits reflect an effort to love myself more and more."

"I am starting to notice a shift in my internal dialogue. I more readily act out of self-love rather than guilt or judgment."

"Every day, I give myself the kind of love and celebration I used to believe was reserved for special occasions."

Week 9 Healing Activities

1. **Morning Celebration Meditation:** Sit down on a comfortable, flat surface, and close your eyes. Begin to breathe fully in through your nose, and out through your mouth. Envision how you want your day to go. Watch the day pass exactly how you want it to. You exude confidence in each activity, and you fully enjoy each moment. Now, envision how you will feel at the end of the day. Feel a warm light come over you as you acknowledge that you worked as hard as you could, appreciated each moment, and made the most of even the smallest tasks. Allow yourself to sit for a few minutes in this warm light, celebrating this great day, knowing that everything is exactly as it should be.

2. **Action Step**: Treating yourself to something nice, just for the sake of it, may feel a bit foreign at first. We are going to practice rewarding ourselves just for being wherever we are on this

journey toward cultivating self-love. Today, treat yourself to your favorite warm beverage in a nice, cozy chair. If it is summer, grab a nice refreshing drink and a seat in the sun. Do not bring your phone or any other distractions. Just sit and enjoy, noticing thoughts that come up and returning to the present. Try to sit and enjoy for at least six minutes.

3. **Celebration Self-hypnosis:** Read this script before you begin, making any adjustments you'd like to create a personal script for your recording. Once you've finished, record yourself saying the script slowly and clearly in an area with no background noise. Pause for at least ten seconds after each line of text to give yourself time for visualization. Lie down in a comfortable position, relax your body, and replay the recording.

"Close your eyes, and breathe in and out calmly. You settle in easily and return to this familiar state of peace. You do this as easily as your breath comes in and goes out.

As you breathe in, you notice an overwhelming sense of joy within you. You breathe out and notice all muscle tension easily melting away.

As you relax more deeply now, you notice you are up on a stage. You feel a gentle breeze gliding along your skin as you calmly peer out in front of you.

Your body feels so relaxed now. You breathe in and out, noticing there is a sea of your favorite people surrounding you in the crowd below. You see your inner self stand up and begin to applaud you.

You feel your body relax as you accept the love that your loved ones, and yourself, extend to you now. You are completely relaxed as you allow joy to spread through every inch of your body.

You allow the emotion and joy to well up as you acknowledge how hard you have worked. You accept this feeling of accepting unconditional love and support coming from yourself and your loved ones.

You feel as if you are floating. Your mind and body are calm and welcome this celebration so readily. You know that you can tap into this feeling at any time.

You are welcoming celebration for your efforts in life with more ease every day. You allow yourself to feel this joy, contentment, and peace growing stronger and stronger.

Welcome yourself back to awareness with a smile. You have earned a bit of celebration for your efforts. You continue to offer yourself this energy as you continue with your day."

Week 9 Reflection

1. Take some time to free-write your thoughts on how this week went. What did you enjoy? What was difficult? Which activities would you like to use again in the future?

2. Once you've reflected a bit about the week,

come up with your own self-celebration affirmation that sums up what you've learned. Try to pick a simple affirmation that can help you get more enjoyment out of the small, everyday tasks in life.

Chapter 10

Breathe Self-Love into Your Routines Moving Forward

"Your beliefs become your thoughts,
Your thoughts become your words,
Your words become your actions,
Your actions become your habits,
Your habits become your values,
Your values become your destiny."

Mahatma Gandhi (Goodreads, 2020)[11]

Now that we've spent several weeks exploring different facets of self-love, you may have already begun incorporating a few self-love practices into your daily routines. Say you're trying to revolutionize your morning routine. You decide you need to wake up two hours earlier than normal, meditate for ten minutes, do yoga for thirty minutes, take a shower, and cook a hot breakfast. The first week you do pretty well, but soon you notice it is difficult to keep up with this goal. Normally you would force yourself to push through with these habits and shame yourself for falling short. However, after exploring self-love a bit, you decide to question this approach.

When creating routines, do you leave a bit of wiggle room for life's inevitable complications?

Does the failure to stick to a new routine cause you to slip out of it altogether?

What do you think a self-loving approach to routines would look like?

When getting curious about your routines, it helps to take a look at your motivators. What are your core reasons for carrying out the routines you've established in your life? Maybe your routines are a result of operating in auto-pilot, and you aren't really sure why you do them. Maybe you guilt-trip yourself into routines that seem healthy on the outside. Maybe your routines truly are continual acts of self-love. Getting to the root of these motivators can help you build routines that feel more achievable, and more loving, in the long-run.

Explore Your Routines

Whether you intentionally created them or not, you already have routines in your life. We may go through the motions of the routines in our lives without questioning why we do the things we do. As we discussed last week, the routines in our lives are another example of seemingly meaningless actions that we can choose to enjoy a bit more. You can learn to care about your routines and honor yourself when completing these actions. Becoming mindful of the way you carry out routines is an act of self-love. When you bring self-love into your routines, you can ensure that you stick with your loving practices, even when you feel busy or overwhelmed. Examine your routines by asking the following questions:

- **Did I intentionally create my routines, or are they made up of actions I do unconsciously?**

- **Does my morning routine set me up for success or leave my feeling stressed out?**

- **Does my evening routine leave my mind rattled and make it difficult to fall asleep, or does it help me relax and unwind both mentally and physically?**

- **Do I have moments in my routines where I am aware, present, and at ease?**

- **Are my routines put in place to force myself into more productivity, or do they include caring efforts to take care of my body and mind?**

Use the questions to gain a bit of awareness regarding your daily routines, but don't get the idea that you need to do a complete routine overhaul. Maybe you're realizing that a lot of your routines could be serving you better, or you spend a good portion of your day in autopilot. Accept this and allow it. If we decide we need to completely redesign our entire lives, we will quickly become overwhelmed and feel like we are failing. This will bring up the shame and guilt tendency we have been trying to undo. The key here is to acknowledge that where you are and where you want to be may be two different places, and that's okay. Your present self still deserves appreciation. Find self-love in taking baby steps and staying consistent with them. Over time, you'll slowly build the momentum needed to create the routines you want.

Weave an Element of Self-Love

So, self-love is in the small gestures, right? But what does this mean, and how do we actually take these steps? These answers will largely depend on you and your goals. But first, consider the idea that it is loving to be gentle with yourself. It is loving to realize that humans need time to change. If you do want to overhaul your routines, it is loving to realize that a significant amount of change will not happen right away. There is love to be found in deciding on one or two daily practices to begin implementing into your daily routine. After a week of consistently completing these steps, you can decide if you are ready to add one more. Your inner self will see these efforts of showing up every single day. Like a child, your inner self will learn, through your actions, that you love yourself.

Here are a few ideas for self-loving routines you can implement at different times of the day. Again, I would recommend choosing one or two to start. Focus on routines that make you feel calm, present, and nurtured in both your mind and body. Maybe start with one new routine in the morning, and another in the evening, and work your way up from there.

Time of Day:	Self-loving Routine Ideas to Incorporate:
Morning: **Before choosing, ask yourself, "Is this achievable and enjoyable?"**	• Meditate for five to ten minutes • Write one page in your journal to check in with yourself mentally • Take five minutes to stretch to check in with yourself physically • Make yourself a warm beverage and take five minutes to enjoy it without screens • Go on a ten-minute walk to energize your body and mind
Commute to work: **Before choosing, ask yourself, "Is this shifting me toward autopilot or awareness?"**	• Check in with your body and your senses. What do you notice about the sights, sounds, and feelings around you? • Listen to a podcast on a topic that excites you • Focus on taking full breaths, and returning to your breath when distracting thoughts come up

Breaks throughout the workday: **Before choosing, ask yourself, "What action would tell my inner self I appreciate their hard work?"**	• Get up to stretch or take a five-minute walk every hour • Take a moment to journal to leave your distracting thoughts on the paper • Make yourself a warm beverage • Take a five-minute meditation break • Take five minutes to research a topic that interests you. Set a timer so you don't spend too much time.
After work: **Before choosing, ask yourself, "What would help me transition from work into a more relaxed mindset?"**	• Change clothes right away and do ten minutes of physical activity • Make yourself and a loved one a snack to enjoy together • Set an alarm to do ten minutes of tidying up • Take ten minutes with no screens, outside if possible

Evening: **Before choosing, ask yourself, "What would put my mind at ease and help my body relax for sleep?"**	• Have a designated time when all screens turn off, preferably two hours before bed • Get in bed half an hour before you want to go to sleep, and spend the extra time reading or meditating • Pay attention to your senses by putting on comfortable clothes, dimming the lights, and turning off any noisy gadgets • Stretch your legs or rub them with a soothing lotion

Self-loving routines allow you to remind yourself that you are loved, without parting from the necessary tasks of your day. You do not need to go on a retreat to weave a tiny amount of self-love into your day. These little efforts of tuning into your body and senses, cultivating presence in your mind, and repeating these steps daily will help you heal and learn to trust yourself. Once you discover activities you adore, repeating them each day will become effortless, yet still remain a meaningful act of self-love.

Acknowledge the Role of Society

Any resistance we feel when incorporating self-love practices may come from what we have learned from society. Society tells us to work harder than expected, turn hobbies into side-hustles, change our bodies, be funnier or more social, be quieter or more mature, and the list goes on. At some point, these external messages become our internal voice, and we learn to tell ourselves over and over again that we need to be different than we are.

This is why consistent self-loving practices are so important. If these messages to question our worth or shame ourselves are so constant, our efforts to shift out of that mindset should also be constant. Practicing self-love reminds you that you deserve acceptance as you are. It helps you to gently push back against the unconscious factors that convince us to judge ourselves or mentally tune out altogether. Remember that your self-love practice is powerful in this sense. As you push back against the feeling that you are undeserving, unworthy, incapable, or flawed, you push yourself toward healing, reconnecting with your inner self, and reconnecting with your loved ones and your community. This effort is not selfish, but vital.

Check in and Maintain Your Efforts

Once you find the ways you enjoy incorporating self-love into your routines, come up with a method for checking in to make sure you are sticking with them. This will be a way you can hold yourself accountable, without pushing yourself too hard or judging yourself when you need to skip a day. Here are a few ideas for self-love check-ins.

- **Have a daily self-love journal entry. Write a couple of lines describing your self-love practice for the day and how it made you feel.**

- **Draw a heart on your calendar after finishing your self-love practice for the day.**

- **Put a sticky note on your mirror or in your workspace, and write a tally mark once you've done your self-love practice for the day.**

- **Set a reminder to check in at the end of each month to write about how your self-love activities went, and how you may want to adjust them for next month.**

The bottom line is, daily self-love matters. But don't forget that some days, self-love may come in the form of forgiving yourself for skipping an activity or slipping up somehow. Return to this idea of showing yourself love, and how it might look different each week, each day, and even each moment. Slowly you'll start to strengthen your inclination toward self-love, and it will become a reflex. You may still have negative thoughts or feelings toward yourself, but you'll be able to shift out of them quicker, and into a more loving place.

Week 10 Daily Affirmations

This week's affirmations remind you to be intentional when creating loving daily routines. They encourage you to see the effort of creating loving routines as an easy and natural process. Use these affirmations to remember that you are creating these routines to treat yourself well. Regardless of your achievements each day, self-love should be the overarching motivator behind your efforts.

"My routines reflect an inner sentiment of self-love."

"I maintain healthy routines with ease because the driving motivator is taking care of myself."

"I am beginning to infuse self-love into every routine in my life. This process feels as easy as breathing."

"I build new routines with ease."

"I honor myself in the routines I create. I check in regularly to make sure they are still serving me well."

"I observe my thoughts to make sure my actions are fueled by a loving and nurturing mindset."

"I make adjustments to my routines effortlessly and without judgment."

Week 10 Healing Activities

1. **Calming Evening Meditation:** Sit or lie down on a comfortable, flat surface and close your eyes. Begin to breathe fully in through your nose, and out through your mouth. Imagine there is a calming lavender colored cloud hovering over your feet. The cloud makes your feet feel extremely heavy and relaxed. Your feet are still and ready to rest for the evening. Allow this cloud to work its way up your body, making your legs, hips, torso, arms, neck, eyelids, and head feel extremely heavy. Eventually, the cloud covers your entire body. Your breath becomes

even slower, and you resign to a restful, peaceful state. As you come back to awareness, you watch the cloud drift away, taking all of your remaining energy with it, and leaving you to sleep your soundest sleep.

2. **Action Step**: This week, pick one or two self-loving efforts that you would like to add to your daily routine. This week, do these new routines every day. Make a journal entry for the seven days to document your progress. In these entries, free write how the activities are going for you. Afterward, answer the following questions:
   - **Are these new routines adding more self-love into my life?**
   - **Are these routines affecting my thoughts throughout the day?**
   - **Do these routines feel difficult or easy? Do I notice any resistance to self-love?**
   - **If these routines are not working, how can I adjust them to make them feel more achievable, or more "me?"**

3. **Self-Love Embodying Hypnosis:** Read this script before you begin, making any adjustments you'd like to create a personal script for your recording. Once you've finished, record yourself saying the script slowly and clearly in an area with no background noise. Pause for at least ten seconds after each line of text, to give yourself time for visualization. Lie down in a comfortable position, relax your body, and replay the recording.

"Breathe in and out, coming to the present with ease, and blinking your eyes until they grow heavy.

As you breathe in, pay attention to any physical sensations you feel. As you breathe out, let go of the sensations and drop into a state of total peace.

As you relax deeper and deeper, you are greeted by your inner self. This familiar friend sits next to you, and you continue to breathe effortlessly.

Your body feels so relaxed and content now. You are drifting deeper and deeper into relaxation. You notice your inner and outer selves begin to merge together as one. This feels like a natural and kind gesture of love. You continue to sink deeper and deeper together.

This union happens as naturally as gravity holds you to the Earth. You accept your inner and outer selves and offer them love so easily now.

I am coming into communion with my inner and outer selves so effortlessly now. This process feels like love. Loving myself feels as easy as floating in a warm bath.

I know my self-love practice is yielding powerful results. I am showing up for myself every day as an act of unconditional love. I feel this sensation at all moments of each day. If I lose the feeling, it quickly comes back as I float back to awareness.

I offer myself love, acceptance, kindness, and trust. I offer these things subconsciously, and with total ease.

I offer myself unconditional love, acceptance, kindness, and trust as I shift back to awareness now. Each time I shift back to awareness, this feeling of self-love comes flooding back to me.

I wiggle my fingers and toes and open my eyes now. I continue to offer myself this love as I continue through my routines, and return to this feeling readily throughout each day."

Week 10 Reflection

1. Take some time to free-write your thoughts on how this week went. What did you enjoy? What was difficult? Which activities would you like to use again in the future?

2. Once you've reflected a bit about the week, come up with your own affirmation that sums up what you've learned about maintaining self-love routines in your daily life. Try to pick a simple affirmation that can remind you of the importance of maintaining your self-love practices every day.

Conclusion

Tying it All Together

*"There is a candle in your heart,
ready to be kindled.
There is a void in your soul, ready to be filled.
You feel it, don't you?"*

Rumi (Goodreads, 2020)[12]

You've made it to the end of this self-love journey! Congratulations! Hopefully by now you have realized a few things about the concept of self-love:

Self-love isn't:	Self-love is:
...an isolated action that you do once and then you are "healed forever!"	...a life long practice that requires a bit of daily action and a lot of self-acceptance.
...required in order for you to give or receive love from others.	...knowing you are worthy of love no matter how much you may struggle to love yourself on any given day.
...a selfish act that takes away from the other connections in your life.	...a necessary act that adds richness and depth to the other connections in your life.
..always as easy as bubble baths and a movie night.	..difficult on some days, but the real love comes from not giving up on yourself in the difficult moments.
...something to shame or guilt yourself into doing.	...something to practice with a mindset of acceptance and ease.
...something that we will have in the future.	...something we have the ability to practice at each moment.

Remember, you deserve love and *are* loved, no matter how you feel at the end of this book. Staying patient and making it to the end of this book was a giant leap toward loving yourself a little bit more every day. This is a practice worthy of your time and energy. By taking this time for yourself, you've shown your inner self that they are worth that time and energy too.

Now that you know you can practice self-love at any moment, I hope you are ending this book with hope for a more loving and kind future. Even if you are still working toward loving yourself better, you have come a long way just by staying persistent, exploring affirmations and hypnosis, and chipping away at the weekly activities and prompts.

Revisiting Our Promises

It's important to revisit the promises we made in the beginning, to recognize just how far we have come on this journey. Do you remember my promise to you at the beginning of this book? Let's revisit it now:

> *"My promise to you is that if you begin this journey from a place of curiosity, kindness, and openness, you will trigger the shift necessary to access a self-love practice."*

I hope you were able to adjust into your self-love practice with ease. However, if you experienced resistance along the way, know that this is normal. Finishing this book is a testament to the fact that you overcame the obstacles, and you still showed up to love yourself anyway. Continue to operate with curiosity, kindness, and openness. Continue to shift out of resistance and judgment, and return back to self-love once again.

What was your promise to yourself? See if you can find where you wrote it down now. Did working toward this promise help you build a more loving relationship with yourself? If the promise didn't work out as planned, were you gentle and forgiving toward yourself anyway? Regardless of how things unfolded, these promises are worth remembering as you continue your self-love practice outside of this book.

Self-Love, Now

Over the course of this book, you've explored the ways you can connect with yourself to begin healing your body and mind. Let's take a look at the topics we've covered over the course of this book.

Finding awareness in the present
Taking care of yourself
Embracing vulnerability
Honoring your authenticity
Building self-trust
Allowing yourself to rest
Cultivating an inner kindness
Constructing a resilient self-image
Celebrating yourself
Maintaining self-loving, consistent routines

These ideas are all central to living in a self-loving way, but they will not always come naturally. Whether you read this book in a few weeks or over the course of a year, you may still find yourself wrestling with a few of these concepts. You may find that some days you are not capable of a single item on this list. And that's okay! The important thing is that you've learned that you can love yourself anyway. It's a great goal to become a self-love guru, but it's arguably even more impressive to acknowledge the difficulty in this practice. Real self-love shows up when you accept yourself, inner demons and all, and continue to offer yourself love anyway. That's what we've started to uncover, and that will be your work moving forward.

Let the Feminine Be

How have you treated the feminine sides of yourself during this process? How has your idea of what it means to be feminine shifted? Every human has feminine qualities. Some of us show them openly, and some suppress them for fear of being perceived as weak or emotional. These elements, such as gentleness, care, intuition, emotion, generosity, wisdom, openness, and vulnerability are difficult to reveal, because they make us feel exposed and raw. We feel others will judge us for showing these sides of ourselves. Hopefully, you've learned to begin embracing these parts of yourself, rather than hiding or fighting them. Doing so is an act of courage. A peace-offering to yourself.

Allowing each part of you, feminine, masculine, neutral, or otherwise, to just be, creates a sense of ease, don't you think? You do not need to be different than you are, and I hope this book has helped you see that. You don't need to hide your emotions, feelings, or whatever else you feel others will dislike about you. Feminine energy is all about being and allowing. Be who you are, and allow that to be enough.

Where to Go From Here

Know that no matter what, this exploration of self-love found you when it was meant to. You may not have been a self-love master before, and you may not be now. In fact, hopefully, now you know that it doesn't even work that way. Self-love isn't something to master, earn a certificate of completion, and move on forever. Self-love is in daily acts of showing up to care for yourself. Self-love is in shifting out of negative thoughts when you feel them creep in. Self-love is acknowledging that you deserve to be treated well, no matter how hopeless you may feel.

In your efforts of meditation, self-hypnosis, journaling, and other action steps, you've begun to form these self-loving habits. Everything you've discovered during these practices is useful information you can use to grow and adjust your personal self-love practices. Continue the daily habits that helped you, and leave behind the ones that didn't fit quite right. The biggest takeaway is knowing that you are worth the time and energy you have put in. You are worth continuing to fine-tune your self-love practice each day, for the rest of your days.

Ending with a Promise

What do you plan to do to continue working on self-love? Take some time to journal about this as your time with this book comes to a close. You can come back to this book whenever you want, but you have the skills necessary to build and maintain your own unique self-love practice. Write down one promise you plan to keep in the days, weeks, months, and years to come. Let this be your first affirmation as you continue on this next step of your journey. As always, I will close with my promise to you.

My promise to you is that you have always had inherent worth, value, and strength. You have always deserved kindness, care, trust, and love. Moving forward with this knowledge, your self-love practice will help you build a deeper relationship with yourself, and the world around you, than you ever imagined."

Here are a few promises you may consider making to yourself now:

- I promise to continue five minutes of self-love journaling every day.
- I promise to continue the meditation and hypnosis practices three days a week.
- I promise to meditate on one self-love affirmation once a week.
- I promise to connect with my inner self through a daily afternoon stroll.
- I promise to adjust my self-love practice daily as it feels appropriate for my body and mind.
- I promise to be a little bit kinder to myself today.
- I promise to do one thing right now that is self-loving.

Once you have decided on a promise, smile, put your hand on your heart, and thank yourself for this effort you have made. Take a moment to acknowledge your progress with a full breath in and out.

Now, close this book and continue your journey, one self-loving step at a time.

Resources

(1) Berry, W., & Meatyard, R. E. (2006). *The Unforeseen Wilderness: Kentucky's Red River Gorge*. Emeryville, CA: Shoemaker Hoard.

(2) A quote by Mother Teresa. (n.d.). Retrieved January 10, 2020, from https://www.goodreads.com/quotes/44552-yesterday-is-gone-tomorrow-has-not-yet-come-we-have

(3) Nhat Hạnh Thich. (2011). *Reconciliation: Healing the Inner Child*. Berkeley, CA: Parallax.

(4) Brown Brené. (2015). *Daring Greatly: How the Courage to be Vulnerable Transforms the Way We Live, Love, Parent, and Lead*. London, England: Penguin Books Ltd.

(5) Tolle, E. (2018). *A New Earth: Awakening to Your Life's Purpose*. London: Penguin Books.

(6) Oliver, M. (2017). *Devotions: the Selected Poems of Mary Oliver.* New York: Penguin Press, an imprint of Penguin Random House LLC.

(7) Angelou, M. (2002). *Wouldn't Take Nothing for My Journey Now.* New York: Random House.

(8) Hay, L. (2017). *You Can Heal Your Life.* Place of publication not identified: Hay House Inc.

(9) A quote by Paulo Coelho. (n.d.). Retrieved February 10, 2020, from https://www.goodreads.com/quotes/94972-and-one-has-to-understand-that-braveness-is-not-the

(10) A quote by Lao Tzu. (n.d.). Retrieved February 23, 2020, from https://www.goodreads.com/quotes/21535-the-journey-of-a-thousand-miles-begins-with-a-single

(11) A quote by Mahatma Gandhi. (n.d.). Retrieved February 28, 2020, from https://www.goodreads.com/quotes/50584-your-beliefs-become-your-thoughts-your-thoughts-become-your-words

(12) A quote by Rumi. (n.d.). Retrieved March 6, 2020, from https://www.goodreads.com/quotes/78367-there-is-a-candle-in-your-heart-ready-to-be

www.ingramcontent.com/pod-product-compliance
Lightning Source LLC
Chambersburg PA
CBHW020905080526
44589CB00011B/457